D1596870

The War of 1812

A Captivating Guide to the Military Conflict between the United States of America and Great Britain That Started during the Napoleonic Wars

Free Bonus from Captivating History (Available for a Limited time)

Hi History Lovers!

Now you have a chance to join our exclusive history list so you can get your first history ebook for free as well as discounts and a potential to get more history books for free! Simply visit the link below to join.

Captivatinghistory.com/ebook

Also, make sure to follow us on Facebook, Twitter and Youtube by searching for Captivating History.

Contents

Introduction

Among all of the conflicts that took place in American history, the War of 1812 is one of the most unique wars that helped to shape many of the important American milestones in the years to come. It was also a battle of surprises and irony as well—firstly, the weaknesses of both parties ultimately ended up being their respective strengths in the two years of constant fighting that started off in 1812. Secondly, the War of 1812 was the most pointless series of conflicts for the parties involved, as the geographical borders ultimately reverted back to what they were before the war, meaning all the resources and manpower that was used or lost during the fighting was all for naught. The War of 1812 was a local war between Canada (which was still under British authority) and the US, as well as a part of the Napoleonic Wars of the early 19th century. In a way, the War of 1812 was a byproduct of the prominent Napoleonic Wars, which was fought mainly in Europe.

With Britain and France competing for control of Europe, both sides understood the importance of disrupting the other side's supply line. And America was smack in the middle of the sea trading routes of both these European nations. The US government saw this as a fortuitous turn of events that would allow them to drive off the British completely from North America and annex Canada as well.

The Americans expected the main British Army to remain occupied in mainland Europe, with only a handful of reserves fighting the battles on the American frontlines. Britain was the largest naval power of the world at that time, and with only a handful of scantily equipped ships and boats holding up the US Navy at that time, the Americans had no illusions of beating the British at sea. Instead, they placed their bets on an overwhelming land victory while the British Army was busy fighting Napoleon's forces.

And this is where the irony kicks in—the American navy ended up winning some improbable victories while suffering some of the most improbable losses when it came to land battles. The one party that ultimately suffered the consequences of the War of 1812 was the Native Americans, but that is a story for another day, one which you can pick up in our American Indian Wars series. In this book, we will take a dive into the various aspects and events of the War of 1812, as well as the impact and aftermath of the events of the war. Despite its short duration, the War of 1812 was very impactful and had a lot of dramatic turns, giving rise to some of the greatest American political and military figures of the 19th century.

Before diving into the specifics of the war, we will first take a look at what brought the war about, as well as an overview of some of the major figures in the war. The War of 1812 saw Generals Andrew Jackson, Jacob Brown, and Winfield Scott rise to prominence, as well as four future presidents—Andrew Jackson, John Quincy Adams, James Monroe, and William Henry Harrison. As this book is split up into the different theaters of the war, a timeline is provided to help the readers understand the bigger picture as well as the smaller details. So, without further ado, let's go ahead!

Chapter One: Prelude to the War

After the British colonies wrested independence through the American Revolutionary War, the fledgling nation still had the worst to face. Beginning with restructuring an economy that was historically dependent on imports and exports with Europe to expanding its own settlements and industries, America had constantly been struggling ever since winning its independence. And despite gaining independence from Britain, frequent clashes and rivalry with the British colonies in Canada was a reality for the US government. Incidents like the famous *Chesapeake-Leopard* affair of 1807 and the *Little Belt* affair of 1811 sparked anger on both sides, which ultimately culminated in the War of 1812. In what was a surprisingly bold move, US President James Madison declared war on June 18th, 1812. All in all, the background of the War of 1812 is far more complicated than it initially seems at first glance due to the various factors involved in the events that led up to it. To have a clearer understanding, we'll have to take a look at some of the events and socio-political changes that occurred between the American Revolutionary War and the War of 1812 that affected both the British and the Americans.

The newly born United States of America was beset with a host of problems after the American Revolution. The war had taken its toll in terms of resources and manpower, requiring the rapid expansion of its borders and settlements to replenish and reinvigorate the economy of the new nation. The new nation had two choices for sustaining itself: trade and expanding its physical territory to gain access to more resources and space. The US saw a boom of immigrants arriving on its shores from different countries in Europe, who were tired of the constant warfare in their own homelands and wanted to pursue a new life. This also opened up opportunities for trade with Europe, especially France. In 1807, at a critical juncture of the Napoleonic Wars, Great Britain proclaimed severe trading restrictions, which greatly angered the Americans. The Order in Councils, which was a bill passed in the British Privy Council, dictated that all neutral countries both inside and outside of Europe needed to obtain permission from Britain to trade with France. This new law affected the US more than anyone, and it rebelled against the bill in 1809 by reestablishing trade with France and blocking trade with Great Britain. Another bill of a similar nature was passed in 1805, known as the Essex Decision, which banned neutral countries of the Napoleonic Wars in trading military items with the French. The US government lashed back at this with the Non-Importation Act. Initially, the US Congress decided not to trade with Britain or France, declaring an embargo against Britain, but seeing how trade was being hampered, it decided to open trade with whichever one of those two superpowers reached out to them by lifting trade restrictions. It was also around this time that many in the US started advocating for war with the British, seeing that they were fully occupied with Napoleon's forces in Europe at the time.

The initial expansion efforts of America were concentrated in the north, which comprises the current-day states of Ohio, Indiana, Illinois, Michigan, and Wisconsin. But their expansion efforts were met with fierce resistance from the Native Americans, who were, for the most part, backed by the British. Even though they had lost the American Revolutionary War, the British influence in the North American continent was far from over. Canada, which was back then a British territory, was a British-Native American buffer zone over which the United States had no control. The British intended to establish a buffer Native American state that would act as a defensive force for its Canadian colonies and protect their trade interests on a long-term basis. However, this directly clashed with the expansionist approach the United States intended to take to expand its border and economy. The Native Americans in the Northwest were putting up an unexpectedly strong opposition against repeated American attempts to establish new settlements. The US military had anticipated that once the American Revolutionary War was over, the British would no longer be able to supply arms and ammunition to the local Native American population, which would make expanding territories easier. But the British managed to keep up the arms influx among the Native American tribes in the north through their trading outposts in Canada. Truth be told, it was the Americans who instigated the Native American tribes first in 1804 by signing a treaty with the Sauk chief Quashquame, who apparently signed off Sauk territory, located in the modern-day states of Missouri and Illinois, to the US government without consent from other chiefs. Many Sauk saw this treaty as unfair and quickly allied themselves with the British to fight for their land. This was followed by the Treaty of Fort Wayne in 1809, which saw the sale of three million acres of land to the US government, paving the way for the states of Illinois and Indiana. A Native American alliance under Tecumseh, a Shawnee chief, started Tecumseh's War following this treaty.

Today, historians universally agree that the US war initiative also intended to annex Canada, ambitiously hoping that the British colonies in Canada would be receptive to independence like they had been. The chief reason for this belief was the fact that a large number of Americans had migrated to Canada at the turn of the 19th century, thanks to fewer taxes on Canadian land. But they didn't turn out to be interested in helping, as most of these emigrants ended up being neutral or apolitical. The Battle of Tippecanoe in 1811 was a turning point for the Native Americans in strengthening their alliance with the British. After this battle, Tecumseh and the major tribal chiefs of the Northwest unanimously came to the conclusion that they needed further British support to defend their lands from the Americans.

This decision further incentivized the Americans to get rid of the British from the continent as soon as possible. However, the War of 1812 was a very divisive war for the US. Half of Congress was against it, and indeed, many Americans at that time referred to the War of 1812 as "Mr. Madison's War," which was harsh to be honest since he was forced to concede to the War Hawks in Washington, who were led by Henry Clay and John C. Calhoun. This particular group of political and military figureheads was only interested in expansion through conquest, and they advocated their agenda to the general public as well as in political circles. Many politicians were reluctant to annex Canada, with some thinking that one side of the US would become too large to control and maintain, while others saw the Canadian colonies and the influence of Catholicism that it would bring, as it was the prominent religion in that region, as being unfit for cohabitating with American values. According to historian Reginald Horsman, annexing Canada was not the end goal for the US but rather a means to an end. The US government knew they had neither the manpower nor resources to keep hold of the extensive stretch of land that is Canada, so their main intention was to use Canada as a bargaining chip to force the British to change their trade policies that hampered their overseas commerce. Other historians, such as Alan Taylor, are of the opinion that annexing Canada was the primary goal of the Americans, as the influential War Hawks in Washington were interested in gaining more territory to build the American economy up. This was reflected in the overturning of a proposed bill to create a provisional government for Canada until the war was over. Before the War of 1812 commenced, many of the War Hawks were of the opinion that America would at least gain Upper Canada, which included all of modern-day Southern Ontario and parts of Northern Ontario, if not the whole territory.

Though trade and expansion were practical reasons, the emotional aspect of British oppression was also a key factor as to why President Madison pushed the bill and why Congress, and eventually the general public, accepted it. While America was officially independent from British rule, it didn't equate to total peace. Even though the British were supposed to pull back from all occupied territory south of the Great Lakes after signing the Treaty of Paris in 1783, they refused to do so until much later in 1795. Then there was also the fact that the British continuously harassed American ships at sea. After the American Revolutionary War, there were many cases of impressment of American sailors into the British Royal Navy. If the reader is unfamiliar with the term, the term impressment means that these men were forced into military service and were basically prisoners of war. Many of these American soldiers were captured from American trading vessels, which greatly outraged many Americans over the years. Then there were the multiple conflicts that took place in the early 1800s, beginning with the *Chesapeake-Leopard* affair of 1807. The *Little Belt* affair of 1811 can be considered the last straw that triggered the demand for war with the British.

It is important to go over these events, as they played a significant role in helping to bring about the war. The *Chesapeake-Leopard* affair took place in 1807 on the coast of Norfolk, Virginia. The HMS *Leopard*, which was tasked with bringing back Royal Navy deserters, chanced upon the American frigate USS *Chesapeake*. After the British warship expressed its intentions to board the *Chesapeake* to search for deserters, the captain of the American frigate refused to allow the British on board. Upon hearing this reply, the HMS *Leopard* opened fire on the *Chesapeake* without warning. After about ten minutes of firing, the British boarded the vessel and took away four Royal Navy deserters and three African Americans, leaving the wreckage and the wounded of the *Chesapeake* without any aid. The incident resulted in the death of three American sailors and eighteen seriously wounded. This turned into a huge diplomatic incident, which forced the British government to offer compensation for the damage caused by the incident, as well as returning the American prisoners. It also played a huge role in reforming and restructuring the US Navy.

The *Little Belt* affair, which occurred a few years later, saw the American frigate USS *President* and the British sloop-of-war, HMS *Little Belt*, engaged with each other. While the reasons behind this incident are unclear, the aftermath is very clear. After the USS *President* cornered the HMS *Little Belt* on the evening of May 16th, 1811, both parties refused to identify each other in the dark of the night. After a few heated words between the captains, a shot was fired; it is unknown who actually shot first. The *Little Belt* was a much smaller ship than the USS *President*, and so, the ship was badly damaged. The British saw nine deaths and 23 injured (two of them dying from their wounds later on), while the Americans only had one injured man. Once the captain of the USS *President* saw the British flags in the morning, he offered aid and shelter to the HMS *Little Belt*, which the British captain promptly refused. The American captain was adamant that the British sloop shot first and that he believed the sloop to be a frigate, due to the angle at which he had approached it. The US government believed the captain, promoting him in rank, which only served to outrage the British even more.

With all of these factors playing out in American politics, it ultimately became inevitable that a major conflict with the British would start. Though the American government painted the War of 1812 as a defensive war, from a socio-political perspective, this war was more about America asserting its independence in front of Europe by humiliating Great Britain than anything else. According to renowned historian H. W. Brands, "The other war hawks spoke of the struggle with Britain as a second war of independence; [Andrew] Jackson, who still bore scars from the first war of independence, held that view with special conviction. The approaching conflict was about violations of American rights, but it was also about vindication of American identity."

Many of the historically accepted causes of the War of 1812 were, in most cases, not as serious as it is often painted out. While impressment by the Royal Navy was indeed a very real problem (almost 10,000 Americans were impressed between 1789 and 1812) and was the main justification of the War Hawks and newspapers to go to war, many of the other reasons weren't as valid. The Native American threat in the Northwest was greatly exaggerated and used as the second prominent reason for annexing Canada, but in all honesty, the situation in the Northwest Territory when it came to Native American conflicts was no different than in other parts of America at that time. The Orders in Council were also commonly cited as another reason to go to war with Britain, but the British Parliament had reverted the order five days before the Americans declared war. As a result, this cause loses its steam in justifying the war. Indeed, considering the widespread opposition against the war, especially in New England, impressment ultimately became the only rallying cry for war at that time.

The Federalist Party was the primary political opposition against the War of 1812. Many state militias were consumed into military service for the war, with many militiamen opposing the enlistment and refusing to enlist. In many cases, such as the British victory at Fort Niagara, militiamen refused to enlist and fight, leading to some resounding defeats.

Chapter Two: Key Players and Statistics of the War of 1812

As in other prior British-American conflicts, the Native Americans also participated in the War of 1812. In fact, a significant number of tribes in the Northwest allied themselves with the British, while a few major Native American tribes allied themselves with the Americans. Surprisingly, the Spanish also participated in the war alongside the British.

It should also be noted that despite the main conflict centering around Great Britain and America, it was the Native Americans who shouldered the highest number of casualties. The Choctaw, Cherokee, Creek, and Seneca tribes fought on the American side. On the other hand, the British had a significantly larger Native American alliance comprised of fourteen tribes— Shawnee, Creek Red Sticks, Ojibwe, Fox, Iroquois, Miami, Mingo, Ottawa, Kickapoo, Delaware (Lenape), Mascouten, Potawatomi, Sauk, and Wyandot—and one confederacy consisting of multiple tribes, Tecumseh's Confederacy. By the end of the War of 1812, all of the tribes on both sides had a combined casualty rate of over 10,000, while the British and Americans were significantly lower. The War of 1812 is also significant for Native Americans because it formally signaled the decline of the power the Native American tribes once held. In fact, the War of 1812 and its impact is often underrated by American and British historians. But for Canadians and Native Americans, this war is a significant part of their history, and they stress its importance even to this day.

One interesting thing to note about the War of 1812 is that when it began, the US Army had a significant advantage in numbers that allowed them to launch a three-pronged attack. But by the end of the war, it was the British who had the advantage in numbers and strategic positioning. At the beginning of the war, the US Army was 7,000 men strong and grew to 35,000 by the end of the war. On the other hand, the British forces were 5,200 strong at the beginning of the war and had 48,000 men by the time it ended. Historians often assume that the British forces would have been much larger had it not been for the Napoleonic Wars. Many of the British at the time didn't even know that the British Empire was engaged at war with the United States until much later. It is estimated that around 16,000 lives were lost in this war; 10,000 Native American casualties, around 3,700 US casualties, and around 2,000 British casualties (although these numbers do vary based on the sources). Another interesting thing to note is that the War of 1812 took place over a large stretch of land and sea despite the small numbers of both sides at the beginning. Despite going against the strongest navy of the world at that time, the US Navy did a terrific job of keeping the Royal Navy in check, capturing 1,400 British merchant ships, whereas the Royal Navy captured 1,344 American merchant ships, throughout the war. Mateo González Manrique, who was the governor of Florida at the time, aided the British with logistics support, thanks to the alliance between the two nations in the Napoleonic Wars.

There were many notable figures participating in this war who would later go on to become important American figures. But not all of them played a significant role in the War of 1812. The key military and political figures that influenced the tides of the War of 1812 can be narrowed down to six names—James Madison (the president of the United States), George Prévost (the governor of Canada), Andrew Jackson (an influential general who would later become a US president), Tecumseh (a Shawnee chief), and Isaac Brock, the tactical and strategic genius who held off the invasion of Canada despite being outnumbered and outgunned.

President James Madison

James Madison, one of the Founding Fathers and the fourth president of the United States, is probably the last person one would envision as a president. He was a man of small stature (standing only 5'5" tall), of meek attitude, and very bookish in nature. Today in American history, he is best remembered as the author of the Constitution. But back in 1812, President Madison was thrust into a political turmoil that would shape American history for decades to come. Born on March 16th, 1751, James Madison was the oldest of the twelve children of James Madison Sr., a wealthy tobacco plantation owner in Virginia. From a very early age, Madison had a delicate health, like most of his siblings who followed him. This restricted his physical activities, such as running and playing outside, at an early age. Instead, he focused on his academics, which he greatly excelled at. Like most children at that time, James Madison went to a local school before going off to college in Princeton. A distinguished academic, Madison graduated from Princeton in 1772, finishing the three-year course in two years. After returning to his family home, Montpelier, he formally entered into the world of politics in 1774.

In many ways, his actions in 1812 can be traced back to this period. Despite not being outspoken, Madison had radical ideas typical of the generation growing up under British tyranny. He felt that despite being subjects of the Crown, America was still socio-economically subjugated by Britain. He was also against the notion of a fixed religion, as he felt that hurt freedom of thought and personal beliefs. His first political position was a stint at the local Committee of

Safety that oversaw the Virginia militia. While he didn't actively participate in the American Revolution, he distinguished himself as an excellent political figure during the war and shone at wartime leadership. From this point onward, Madison's rise in politics was steady and unbroken. He served in Congress from 1780 to 1783, and he won a seat in the Virginia House of Delegates the following year in 1784. In 1789, he ran against James Monroe for a seat in the US House of Representatives, winning the election. He went on to serve under the Washington, Adams, and Jefferson presidencies and made many necessary changes to the US Constitution to ensure the personal liberties and rights of US citizens.

Madison became the secretary of state in 1801 during President Thomas Jefferson's tenure, a position which he served until 1808. As mentioned, James Madison won the fourth US presidential election in 1808 and was inaugurated in the position the following year. Serving in the position for eight years, President Madison had a very busy time. The first quarter of his presidency was spent fighting the War of 1812, while during the latter half, he had to make important constitutional changes to silence critics and opponents vocal of his policies. In many cases, he accepted the policies he once opposed, stabilizing the increasingly unstable American political environment at that time. After stepping down from the presidency, Madison retired to his family home, Montpelier, Virginia. He never actively participated in politics for the rest of his life except for one more time in 1829 when he helped to revise the constitution of Virginia. James Madison passed away on June 28th, 1836, at the age of 85. Despite his best efforts, his legacy is a failed one, with most historians critical of his competency and leadership, especially during the War of 1812.

George Prévost

Commonly referred to as the "Defender of Canada" in Canada's history, George Prévost was the brainchild in planning the Canadian defense strategy during the War of 1812. Born on May 19th, 1767, George Prévost was the oldest son of Augustine Prévost, a British officer who came to America in 1765. Like many other major figures involved in the War of 1812, little is known of his childhood except that he was born in Hackensack, New Jersey, and was of Genevan origin and spent his youth partially in England for schooling. Official records of his life start from his military service in 1779. George Prévost was somewhat of a prodigy, entering his father's unit at the age of only eleven, joining as an ensign. By the age of fourteen, young Prévost was a full-fledged lieutenant and had been transferred to the 47th Regiment of Foot.

During the next few years, Prévost slowly ascended through the British ranks, most likely due to his grandfather buying his promotions, which was a somewhat common practice at the time. Despite these commissioned promotions, Prévost proved himself valiantly in the French Revolutionary Wars in 1792 at the age of 23. After four years of service, he was promoted to the rank of colonel and assigned to the West Indies. This was where his political and leadership skills were honed, as he was appointed as the administrator of the island of St. Lucia and later Dominica. He successfully defended his territory and retired to England in 1805. After three years of respite, George Prévost was appointed as the governor of Nova Scotia in 1808, along with the rank of lieutenant general, due to his immense administrative success in the Caribbean. From the get-go, George Prévost made radical and quick changes in both the economic and military infrastructure of the region, which immensely benefited from them. He fortified the defenses of Nova Scotia and coordinated the local militia with the British military. These are the chief reasons why the American forces repeatedly failed in their Canadian conquest a few years down the line. In 1809, Prévost coordinated the invasion of Martinique, which was led by William Cottnam Tonge, his political opponent. By making him second-in-command of the Martinique invasion, Prévost hoped to win over Tonge, as well as gain support in the House of Assembly, which Tonge was a part of.

In July 1811, due to his administrative and military successes, George Prévost was appointed as the governor and commander-in-chief of British North America and its military forces. As such, he also took control of Lower Canada (a region that covered the southern portion of the current-day Province of Quebec and the Labrador region of the modern-day Province of Newfoundland and Labrador), which had been under the authority of Thomas Dunn. By the time he was single-handedly managing Canada, Prévost had realized that he couldn't afford a revolutionary war, which was what the Americans wanted and which was something that was becoming more of a possibility. So, he started including more Canadian natives in government positions and the Legislative Council, which greatly bolstered his popularity. Once the War of 1812 started, Prévost found himself in a difficult position, despite anticipating the war, due to a lack of manpower and resources. In the initial American attack in 1812, Major General Isaac Brock successfully carried out Prévost's defensive plans and beat back the Americans at the cost of his own life. By 1813, Britain had realized the importance of the war in North America and sent in Commodore Sir James Yeo to defend the Great Lakes region due to its strategic importance. Combining forces, Yeo and Prévost attacked New York, but the British forces were beaten back by Brigadier General Jacob Brown's forces. This defeat was followed by another one on the waters of Lake Erie. But in the end, his forces ultimately managed to beat the second American invasion in Canada at Chateauguay and Crysler's Farm near Montreal.

Prévost's fortune soured again in 1814 when the Americans saw major success in the Capture of Niagara. But fortunately for Prévost, Napoleon's defeat that spring meant that the British could finally afford to send their veteran troops to North America. After receiving 15,000 men in reinforcements, Prévost started to plan the Plattsburgh campaign. Since we will be discussing the American invasion of Canada in more detail later in the book, we'll skip any discussion over it here, except for the fact that Prévost withdrew his forces to Canada at the last moment.

Due to his refusal to engage with the Americans, Prévost was relieved of his position as governor. Shortly after stepping down as the governor of British North America, he was severely criticized for his refusal to engage with the enemy in the Plattsburgh campaign. Furthermore, Yeo also made a negative report of Prévost's actions throughout the war, which further diminished his reputation. This, coupled with his ill health, which had been an issue since the end of the War of 1812, took its toll and resulted in his death on January 5th, 1816, one month prior to his court-martial hearing to clear his reputation. Though he died disgraced and shamed at the end of his life, Prévost is revered by Canadians today as Canada's guardian angel in its infancy.

Andrew Jackson

By all accounts, Andrew Jackson, who would one day be the seventh president of the US, was a living legend during his lifetime and is still considered so today. An accomplished soldier and statesman, Jackson rose to fame through his military exploits and won the heart of his countrymen by standing for the rights of the common man. Andrew Jackson's military exploits began with the War of 1812, so one could say that this war shaped Andrew Jackson's military and political career.

Andrew Jackson was born on March 15th, 1767, in the Waxhaw Settlement, located between modern-day North Carolina and South Carolina, and he was the youngest of three children. His parents, Andrew and Elizabeth Hutchinson Jackson, emigrated from Northern Ireland to the US shortly before his birth. As he was born to a fairly poor family, Jackson seems to have had precious little education, and little is known about his childhood. It is known that his father died in an accident before he was born and that Jackson's eldest brother participated in the American Revolutionary War, dying in the Battle of Stono Ferry in 1779. Probably due to her Irish grit, Elizabeth Jackson seemed to have been unfazed at this loss and encouraged her other two sons, Robert and Andrew, to join the local militia. Under Colonel William Richardson Davie, the two brothers served as couriers due to their tender age, but tragedy befell the family in 1781. After disobeying British troops in a raid, both boys were deliberately imprisoned, where they contracted smallpox. Robert died after his release, and his mother followed shortly after while serving as a volunteer nurse in Charlestown harbor. Left alone in the world, a fourteen-year-old Andrew Jackson blamed the British for his family misfortune and cultivated a rage that, while unhealthy, served him well in his military endeavors. But this same trait also brought him under fire in his personal life, which is filled with controversy even today.

After the war, young Andrew Jackson drifted from one profession to another until encountering attorney Spruce Macay in South Carolina, who took him under his wing. After spending some time under Macay's tutelage, Jackson became eligible to qualify for the bar, officially starting his career as a lawyer in 1787. After starting his new career, he got himself into a socially controversial position for getting involved in an affair with his future wife, Rachel Donelson, at whose mother's house he was boarding at that time. The duo married in 1790, but the stigma of the controversy remained for a long time. For the first few years of his career, he kept clear of politics, focusing on his career growth. But in the mid-1790s, he saw a meteoric rise in politics. He went on to serve in the Tennessee constitutional convention in 1796 and was accepted into the Democratic-Republican Party (which was known as the Republican Party at the time; this party had nothing to do with the current two major US political parties, although one faction of this party did eventually turn into the Democratic Party).

The following year, he was elected as a US senator, a position that he turned down very quickly due to strongly disagreeing with President Adams' administration. This won him strong political support back in Tennessee, where he was elected as a judge for the

Tennessee Supreme Court. He also became a judge advocate of the Tennessee militia. But his political achievements were short-lived, as he again got entangled in a political controversy known as the Sevier affair. In 1802, Jackson announced his candidacy for major general of the Tennessee militia, a position that John Sevier had his eyes on. The two tied, and the governor broke the tie in Jackson's favor, perhaps due to evidence of land fraud that Jackson brought the governor's attention to. In 1803, Sevier announced his intentions to run for the post again, and the governor released the information, with Jackson following up on that with a scathing newspaper article on Sevier's character; the two almost got into a duel over the matter.

Jackson did end up in a duel later on in life. In 1806, Jackson's rival, Charles Dickinson, wrote an article, slandering his wife Rachel, a sore point for Jackson. Jackson then decided to engage in a duel with Dickinson, who was a noted attorney and a famous duelist. Instead of maintaining the standard custom of both duelists drawing at the same time, Jackson braved his opponent's bullet first then deliberately aimed and killed his opponent; back then, firing a second shot was not allowed, unlike the cowboy duels popularized by movies. This, added with his habit of cheaply undermining political opponents, his radical political notions, and elitist views on slavery, made him a social outcast outside his military and political circles. Jackson tried to regain some of his social standing by aligning with Aaron Burr but ultimately ended up betraying him after learning of Burr's true intentions, as he wanted to create a new empire to compete with the US.

It wasn't until 1813, almost a year after the War of 1812 had been declared, that Jackson actively participated in the war. He first served under General James Wilkinson, which didn't pan out too well as Jackson was forced to disband his militia forces and turn his supplies to General Wilkinson without even fighting a battle. But Jackson's turn to shine came during the Creek War, which started on August 30th, 1813. In October of the same year, Jackson, leading 2,500 men, established Fort Strother in the Mississippi Territory and went on to win the Battle of Tallushatchee and the Battle of Talladega by the following month. After surviving a harsh winter, Jackson and his forces were set back by the Red Sticks in the Battles of Emuckfaw and Enotachopo Creek. But he bounced back with the Battle of Horseshoe Bend in March 1814 and went on to enforce the Treaty of Fort Jackson, which ended the Creek War, under President Madison's orders.

Following this victory, Jackson decided to corner the British in Spanish Florida, hoping to take the region and beat the British at the same time. But the British had successfully baited Jackson with Spanish Florida while preparing to attack New Orleans. When Jackson realized his mistake, he immediately abandoned Pensacola to travel to New Orleans. The Battle of New Orleans, while commonly considered Jackson's crowning achievement, is now controversially viewed by historians. The main reason for the controversy is that by the time Jackson had taken over the city, the Treaty of Ghent, which ended the War of 1812, had already been signed. Also, he had turned into a despot while occupying New Orleans. The first reason doesn't stand strong, as letters from British Secretary of War Henry Bathurst to Major General Sir Edward Pakenham, who had been given the command to take New Orleans, ordered him to continue full-scale war despite the Treaty of Ghent. But after Jackson's victory over the British forces on January 8th, 1815, Jackson declared total martial law in New Orleans, which saw the total subjugation of civil rights. He went on to be a major figure in the First Seminole War, which again saw him mired in controversy for attacking the Spanish in Pensacola without provocation.

In 1828, Jackson ran for president and won the election, largely thanks to his military achievements in the War of 1812 and the First Seminole War. Andrew Jackson's presidency was a controversial one due to his extreme political views. Some of them were controversial during his own lifetime, like the Specie Circular (which required payment for land to be made in gold and silver and which led to an economic panic) and the Petticoat affair, which shaped the future American feminist movement, while others, like the Native American removal policy, became controversial after his death. He stepped down from office in 1837 after serving two terms as the US president but continued to be active in politics until his death in 1845. It should be noted that despite the many controversies surrounding this American legend, his presidency is considered to be one of the most successful ones in US history, thanks to many of his reformation policies.

Tecumseh

In a way, Tecumseh was the last great Native American visionary. While there were many notable Native American figures long after his death, all of them fought to keep the rights and integrity of their people. Tecumseh, on the other hand, envisioned a confederacy of Native American nations, which was not too different from George Washington's vision. Born in present-day Ohio, in 1768, the exact place of Tecumseh's birth is undetermined. His father, Puckshinwa, was a respected Shawnee chief, and as such, Tecumseh was groomed to be a leader from an early age. After the death of his father in the Battle of Point Pleasant in 1774 at the hands of the Virginia Militia, his mother left him and his other siblings to the care of Tecumseh's older sister to move back with her own tribe. Tecumseh was only seven years old at that time. In the absence of his father, his older brother, Chiksika, took over his training. When he grew older, the famous Shawnee chief Blackfish adopted him into his tribe.

Tecumseh went on his first raid against the American settlers when he was only fourteen years old. His first skirmishes were during the American Revolutionary War, in which he proved himself a capable warrior. Despite his hate against the Westerners for killing his father, Tecumseh approached warfare in a very civil manner. He condoned acts of cruelty and criticized his peers for doing so. After the American Revolutionary War, Tecumseh took part in many small raids on behalf of the Wabash Confederacy, becoming the chief of the Kispoko division of the Shawnee in 1792. After the Treaty of

Greenville was signed in 1795, Tecumseh settled down briefly, taking a Shawnee woman named Mamate as his wife, who bore him a son named Paukeesaa. Sadly, their marriage did not last, and the sister who had taken care of Tecumseh when he was young began to raise Paukeesaa when he was about seven. Tecumseh was extremely opposed to the Treaty of Greenville and called out the Shawnee chiefs who had signed the treaty for temporary provisions.

Over the next nine years, Tecumseh led a quiet existence until his younger brother, Tenskwatawa, became famous as the Prophet. Around 1805, Tecumseh settled in Greenville, Ohio, where he started building up the military might of the Native American nations using his brother's influence. Tecumseh's dream of a Native American alliance also bloomed during this time. Using his brother's influence as a rallying call, Tecumseh hoped to establish the great Native American confederacy that he dreamed of. Tenskwatawa's teachings were simple—those who followed his lessons were to go back to the days before the white settlers came, and in order to do this, the Native Americans needed to give up Western vices and hedonism and turn back to the old spiritual ways of their peoples. His movement gained much traction, and within a short while, people from all tribes were flocking to his village to meet him. But there were also those among the Native Americans who opposed Tenskwatawa's rising influence due to the brutality he inflicted on those he deemed as sinners. However, by 1808, the village had gotten so large that Tecumseh and Tenskwatawa decided to relocate their base of operations somewhere the Americans couldn't attack easily. This was a smart assumption as the Shawnee relations with the US government continued to deteriorate with the more influence Tenskwatawa gathered. So, they moved farther west down the Wabash and Tippecanoe Rivers and established Prophetstown, one of the largest multi-tribe Native American camps in Native American history.

In 1810, Tecumseh's clash with the Americans officially started, which marked the beginning of Tecumseh's War. Initially,

Tecumseh and William Henry Harrison were supposed to meet for peace talks in Vincennes in August 1810. Even though it was agreed upon that Tecumseh would go there with a small detachment of bodyguards, Tecumseh decided to make an appearance with a large force to throw Harrison off guard. Naturally, this did not sit well with Harrison, and the ensuing conversation almost turned into a full-blown fight, with both parties leaving before anything unpleasant happened. Tecumseh argued that the Native American tribes constituted one nation and that the Miami alone didn't have the right to sell the land allotted in the treaty. Harrison disputed this claim by pointing out that Native American tribes historically always held different alliances with Westerners and did not speak a common language nor shared a common culture. Since Harrison couldn't understand Tecumseh, he allowed him to speak, not realizing that Tecumseh was beginning to encourage his men to attack him. However, Harrison and his men left before things went too far, but the damage had been.

With Tenskwatawa serving as the spiritual leader and Tecumseh as the military leader, Tecumseh's dream of a unified Native American coalition was almost realized, but it sadly failed. While Tecumseh was away rallying other tribal leaders for the coalition, William Henry Harrison led his forces on Prophetstown on November 7th, 1811, in the Battle of Tippecanoe. Instead of retreating as he should have, Tenskwatawa decided to lead the battle against the attackers, hoping to emulate his brother's bravery on the battlefield. But he was soundly defeated, and with the fall of Prophetstown, Tecumseh's dreams were dashed as well.

After this crushing defeat, Tecumseh quickly allied himself with the British to gain access to weapons and supplies he desperately needed to fight back against the Americans. He ended up allying himself with Isaac Brock, and the two men established a functional alliance to help each other out. Tecumseh's forces knew the lay of the land and were adept at guerilla attacks, harassing the American forces and often cutting them off from supplies and communication lines, a tactic that made the first American invasion into Canada a total disaster. Tecumseh participated in the Siege of Detroit, along with Isaac Brock, in 1812, and they followed that victory with the Siege of Fort Meigs in 1813. After Brock's death, Tecumseh joined with Colonel Henry Procter in the Battle of the Thames, but the alliance ultimately didn't turn out to be very effective. While Tecumseh had a cordial and respectful relationship with Brock, that was not the case with Procter. The two men were at odds with what strategy to follow and decided to attack separately. Tecumseh led an ill-advised charge against the American forces, which resulted in his untimely death. His body was never properly identified, but one body that closely matched his physical description (including his lifelong limp) indicated injuries that would have resulted in immediate death.

Tecumseh's death was a huge blow for the Native Americans as a whole in the 19th century. Those among the Native American tribes who opposed him soon realized their folly in the decades following his death, as one tribe after another was pushed onto Native American reservations.

Isaac Brock

While George Prévost created the plans for Canada's defense in the War of 1812, it was Isaac Brock who realized those plans in reality. Energetic, popular, and ambitious, Isaac Brock wanted fame and glory that only European wars could bring. He believed that by proving his merit in the North American conflicts that he would be eventually transferred to European frontiers like in his youth. Isaac Brock was born on the British Channel Island of Guernsey on October 6th, 1789. His father was a sailor in the Royal Navy, and naturally, he followed in his father's footsteps once he got older. Despite his short schooling, Brock had an unquenchable thirst for knowledge and was a voracious reader throughout his life. Brock joined his brother in the 8th Regiment of Foot at the age of fifteen and made his way to the rank of lieutenant by 1790, buying the ranks as Prévost had. The following year, Brock was promoted to the rank of captain and gained command of his own company. After a short two-year stint in the Caribbean, Brock fell ill, nearly dying, and returned to England in 1793.

After a few years, Brock commanded the 49th Regiment in the War of the Second Coalition (a war fought against revolutionary France) in 1798 in the Batavian Republic. He fought in Europe for four years before being assigned to Canada in 1802. Instead of fighting on the frontlines, Brock found himself dealing with internal disputes, such as desertion and mutiny. For an adventurer and risk-taker of the highest caliber, there couldn't be a worst fate than this. There is a story about Brock and a duelist when he joined the 49th Regiment. The duelist was an officer in the same regiment and supposedly insulted Brock badly enough that a pistol duel was called for. When the conditions of the duel were to be set, Brock demanded that they fire standing away the length of a handkerchief from each other. Hearing this condition, Brock's opponent gave up on the duel and retired from the regiment.

After his arrival in Canada, Brock was vocal about improving Canada's defenses, something that would greatly benefit the region. Despite his best efforts, support and supplies in Canada were scarce, and Brock longed to be back in the European theater of the Napoleonic Wars. Instead of heeding his repeated requests, he was given more responsibility, becoming the administrator of Upper Canada along with a promotion to major general. It was during this time that Brock solidified his alliance with the Native Americans, who would go on to become his allies in the War of 1812. Despite all of these preparations, Brock was caught off guard when war was declared by the Americans in June 1812. He only had 1,200 regulars at his disposal. Even though he had restructured the Canadian militia, he didn't trust the Canadians to be as effective and loyal as his British regulars. Despite his misgivings, he decided to trust Captain Charles Roberts, who was in charge of a ragtag band of regulars, frontiersmen, and Native Americans, to attack Fort Mackinac if he deemed it possible. Captain Roberts proved himself to be very capable, taking over the American fort with ease (it probably helped that the men stationed at the fort didn't even know that war had been declared). This victory encouraged the Native Americans who were still neutral to ally themselves with the British.

Initially, Brock and George Prévost were at odds with each other in handling the defense of Canada. While Brock wanted to take advantage of the momentum of Robert's victory at Fort Mackinac and push back the Americans, Prévost, who had yet to take the office of governor, wanted to wait things out until he arrived on the scene. But the American forces didn't adhere to his timing and forced Brock into action when Brigadier General William Hull moved on Canada from Detroit on July 11th. Though the Americans retreated, Brock pressed forward with around 400 men, intending to crush the American forces. Tecumseh himself joined Brock with 600 warriors in Amherstburg on August 13th. Combining their forces together, the two capable commanders successfully laid siege to Fort Detroit, winning a stunning victory three days later despite being outnumbered. Tecumseh was so impressed with Brock that despite some minor differences with Brock, he praised and respected Brock for being "a real man." Brock even promised a negotiation with the Shawnee without overpromising anything—many historians assume that had Brock lived, the fate of the Native American nations in the 19th century might have turned out differently.

Despite these early successes, which definitely impacted American morale, Isaac Brock did not live long enough to see the fruits of his success. Shortly after the first wave of invasion, the Madison administration decided to send in the second wave to conquer Canada by crossing the Niagara River. This time, the American forces were led by American General Stephen Van Rensselaer III. When the Battle of Queenston Heights began on October 13th, 1812, Brock was still not on the battlefield yet. By the time he had reached Queenston Heights, the American forces had successfully crossed the Niagara and were fighting to take control of the Canadian side of the river, forcing Brock and his forces to retreat. Fearing the Americans might break through, Brock immediately led a counterattack to push back the US forces. Despite his brave efforts, Brock ultimately fell in battle in the middle of the charge after being severely wounded once. After his death, and that of the subsequent commander, the British troops pulled back until Major General Roger Sheaffe arrived and defeated the American forces.

Three days after his death, Major General Isaac Brock was buried at Fort George on October 16th, 1812. Nearly 5,000 people attended his funeral, an astounding number considering the spread of the Canadian population at that time. Canadians, British, and Native Americans all came to pay their final respects to the fallen hero. While Isaac Brock's death was a crushing defeat, it helped spark an intense fighting spirit within the Canadian forces for the rest of the War of 1812.

Chapter Three: Timeline of the War of 1812

Since the War of 1812 took place in multiple theaters, the sequence of events described in this book might be disorienting for many readers considering the length of the book as well as the way the events are categorized. There's also the fact that there are so many events in the War of 1812 that are of major and minor importance that fitting all of them into one short book is not possible. To make things easier for our readers, here is a rundown of the main events of the War of 1812, including the events that led up to the war, before delving further into the topic. If at any point you feel confused about the sequence of events, feel free to browse through this chapter. Also included are some minor incidents that were not covered extensively in this book.

1803

April 30 – The Louisiana Purchase Treaty is signed, which allowed the US to gain the territory of Louisiana from France. The Louisiana Purchase added more than 800,000 square miles to the western frontier of the United States, substantially increasing its geographical boundaries in the west.

1804

December 2 – Napoleon is crowned Emperor of France. Although the start date of the Napoleonic Wars is debated among historians, some agree that this is the beginning of the wars.

1805

May 22 – The Essex Decision is passed in the British Parliament to prevent France from gaining overseas supplies. This law dictated that only civilian products could be traded during wartime in British waters, effectively banning weapons and military supply trading.

1806

April 18 – The Non-Importation Act is passed by the Americans in response to the trade restriction law imposed by the British to cut off trade with France and its allies. This act did not have as much of an impact as American politicians desired.

November 21 – The Berlin Decree is issued by Napoleon to impose a blockade on the British so they would be cut off from trade with mainland Europe.

1807

June 22 – The *Chesapeake-Leopard* Affair takes place, which causes outrage among the American public.

November 11 – The Orders in Council are passed by Great Britain, which further restrict international trade between France and its allies, along with the rest of the world (it should be noted the first order was passed on January 6th). The Americans were the most heavily impacted because it was the only major neutral country trading with Europe at that time.

December 22 – The Embargo Act is passed by the US Congress. Tired of the British and French trade restrictions, the US decided to stop all trade with Europe. This hurt their economy badly and was reverted soon after.

1809

March 1 – The Non-Intercourse Act, which replaced the Embargo Act, is passed in Congress. Congress decided to commence trading with all European countries except Great Britain and France, hoping to reinvigorate the US economy. This act was passed during the last days of President Jefferson's tenure and ultimately ended up in failure.

March 4 – President Jefferson steps down from office, and James Madison is sworn in as the fourth president of the United States. Due to the intense political and economic situation of the US, President Madison had to take crucial actions immediately.

September 30 – The Treaty of Fort Wayne is signed. Also known as the Twelve Mile Line Treaty, this treaty saw the US government purchase three million acres of land from Native American tribes living in present-day Indiana and Illinois. This treaty helped precipitate Tecumseh's War.

1810

May 1 – Macon's Bill Number 2 is signed into law by President Madison. With the French and British trade restrictions in place, American ships were being captured left and right by both powers. Since the Embargo Act and the Non-Intercourse Act proved to be ineffective, this bill was proposed in early 1810 to put an end to this problem, which was costing the Americans a lot, despite being neutral. The new bill saw the Americans opening trade with both the French and the British again, with a warning that whoever violated the rights of the US would find themselves facing America as their enemy. Napoleon feigned signs of interest in an alliance but ultimately backed off. While the Americans got the French off their back, handling the British was an entirely different story. Angered at the perceived arrogance of the Americans, the British doubled down on harassing American merchant ships. This further gave the War Hawks in Washington the reasons they needed to stir up outrage in the newspapers.

August, date unspecified- The beginning of Tecumseh's War.

1811

February 2 –American trade with Britain is formally closed. This time, the economic cut-off was permanent until the War of 1812 ended.

May 16 – The Little Belt affair takes place, making it the last controversial conflict that finalized the inevitability of the War of 1812.

October 9 – Major General Isaac Brock is appointed as the administrator of Upper Canada.

November 7 – The Battle of Tippecanoe takes place. This defeat dismantled all the work that Tecumseh had been focusing on to build up a Native American confederacy.

1812

June 16 – Great Britain withdraws the Orders of Council, which restricted American trade. One could say that this decision came too little too late. The Americans declared war two days later, and it is doubtful whether receiving this news would have changed their decision.

June 18 – The United States declares war on Britain by invading Canada. President Madison deduced that by capturing Canada before the British could respond, the American military would be able to handicap the Royal Navy by denying them the timber supplies required to build their ships.

June 22 – In Baltimore, the printing offices of the newspaper *Federal Republican*, a publication that was against the war, is destroyed by a mob. The owner of the newspaper, Alexander Contee Hanson, voiced concerns that America was not well equipped for the war and warned the demise of the United States if it participated in a full-fledged war against Britain. The general sentiment in Baltimore was pro-war, so this did not sit well with the general populace. The mob attacked Hanson and his friends, who escaped to a jail temporarily, but the mob broke in and assaulted the men with knives and clubs. Hanson was left for dead while another friend, who was a general in the militia, was killed by the mob.

July 12 – General William Hull crosses the Detroit River and makes it to Canada. This was part of the three-wave invasion plan devised by the US Army to take over Canada from three sides.

July 17 – Fort Mackinac surrenders to the British-Canadian-Native American forces without even firing a shot. This was the first major land engagement of the war, and this victory swayed over the Native American tribes who had not allied themselves with the British yet.

July 19 – The First Battle of Sacket's Harbor takes place. As it was an important naval strategic position for the American Navy, Sacket's Harbor was attacked twice by the British forces in the War of 1812. The first attack was led by the Royal Navy, which the Americans beat back easily.

August 5 – The Battle of Brownstown.

August 9 – The Battle of Maguaga. This battle is often considered to have started due to both sides accidentally stumbling upon each other.

August 15–August 16 – The Siege of Fort Detroit. Despite being outnumbered, the British-Canadian-Native American forces won an overwhelming victory that dealt a serious blow to the American forces and morale.

August 15 – The Battle of Fort Dearborn.

August 19 – The USS *Constitution* defeats the HMS *Guerriere*. While not a full-scale naval battle, it was the first American victory in the War of 1812, which helped to increase American morale

September 3 –The massacre at Pigeon Roost takes place. Arguably the first massacre of the War of 1812, a group of Shawnees, and possibly some Delawares and Potawatomis, attacked the small village of Pigeon Roost, killing 24 settlers, 15 of whom were children.

September 5 –   First siege of Fort Madison.

September 5–September 12 –   The Siege of Fort Wayne, which saw the first major Native American loss in the War of 1812.

September 21 –   The Raid on Gananoque, located in Upper Canada.

October 13 – The Battle of Queenston Heights, located in Ontario. Major General Isaac Brock died in this battle.

October 18 – The Americans of the USS *Wasp* capture the HMS *Frolic*. The British had 15 killed and 43 wounded, while the Americans had 5 killed and 5 wounded. However, the Royal Navy retaliated the same day and took back the captured ship, as well as the USS *Wasp*.

November 23 –   The Americans retreat from Eastern Canada after the first wave of invading Canada failed. This doesn't mean they gave up on the invasion—rather, they were trying to save resources.

November 10 – The American navy leads an attack on Kingston Harbor, which was an important Canadian port.

November 22 – The Battle of Wild Cat Creek.

November 28 –   The Battle of Frenchman's Creek.

December 17–18 –The Battle of the Mississinewa.

December 28 – William Henry Harrison resigns as the governor of the Indiana Territory and instead becomes a brigadier general.

December 29 – The USS *Constitution* defeats the HMS *Java*. Just a little before Christmas, the USS *Constitution* came upon the HMS

Java as it was patrolling the coast of Brazil. Both frigates entered into a short skirmish that ended up with the HMS *Java* surrendering.

1813

January 9 – Great Britain declares war on the United States. While the British had already been at war with the Americans for a while, they hadn't publicly announced the war. On this day, the official declaration of the War of 1812 was announced in Britain. Canada also started receiving more mainland military support from Britain after the declaration.

January 13 – John Armstrong replaces William Eustis as the US secretary of war. A hero of the American Revolution, Armstrong was well into retirement when he was recalled for duty by the US government. He was instrumental in organizing the US Army but is most noted for his failure to defend Washington, D.C., in the War of 1812.

January 18–23 – The Battle of Frenchtown, also known as the Battle of the River Raisin or the River Raisin Massacre. This battle had the highest casualty rate for the American forces in the War of 1812 in a single battle. Four hundred and ten Kentucky militiamen died in this battle, while the British-Canadian forces had 25 recorded deaths.

February 22 – The Battle of Ogdensburg takes place. Ogdensburg was an important supply outpost for the American forces in New York. The British attacked this small village and took it over, eliminating a direct threat to the British supply lines toward the beginning of the war.

April 27 – The Battle of York, located in modern-day Toronto, takes place. US Brigadier General Zebulon Pike is killed in this battle.

April 29 – The raid on Frenchtown, Maryland, by a British armada commanded by Rear Admiral George Cockburn, takes place. This success gave Cockburn reason to continue venturing along Elk River.

March 4 – James Madison is inaugurated for his second term as president.

April 28–May 9 – The Siege of Fort Meigs, located in modern-day Perrysburg, Ohio, takes place. The siege didn't officially start until May 1ˢᵗ. Despite their best efforts, the British forces failed to capture the fort and were forced to withdraw.

May 3 – The raid on Havre de Grace, Maryland, was quite unique, as there was only one casualty in this raid. But the burning of Havre De Grace made the Americans both fearful and resentful of the opposition.

May 25–27 – The Battle of Fort George takes place. This was one of the earliest and biggest American victories in Upper Canada. Leading an amphibious assault, comprising of both small gunboats and infantry, Oliver Hazard Perry and Henry Dearborn won an overwhelming victory. This pattern was also replicated in a few other American victories.

May 28–29 – The Second Battle of Sacket's Harbor takes place. After a ten-month gap, the British forces attacked Sacket's Harbor for the second time to no avail. The American forces once again repelled the British forces led by George Prévost and James Lucas Yeo. While the British had more dead and wounded soldiers, they managed to capture 154 Americans during the battle.

June 1 – The USS *Chesapeake* is captured by the British frigate HMS *Shannon*; this skirmish is also known as the Battle of Boston Harbor. A short and brutal battle, the US and British forces fought for about fifteen minutes, which resulted in 71 (23 British and 48 American) casualties and the capture of the USS *Chesapeake*. Captain James Lawrence died three days later due to his wounds.

June 6 – The Battle of Stoney Creek takes place. This was a decisive victory for the British-Canadian forces under Colonel John Harvey, who saw the Americans driven out of Upper Canada permanently. Despite taking heavy casualties, the British-Canadian forces captured the enemy commanders, throwing the American forces into disarray.

June 22 – The Battle of Craney Island takes place. This was a rousing win for the Americans, who saw the British naval forces led by Rear Admiral George Cockburn retreat with about 200 casualties. Besides defending Norfolk, which was the main objective of the British forces, this battle essentially discouraged any major British naval initiative in the region for the rest of the War of 1812.

June 24 – The Battle of Beaver Dams takes place. This is also the source of the Canadian legend of Laura Secord's heroic journey from Queenston to the DeCew House to warn the British of a surprise attack by the Americans. The American forces initially had the element of surprise, but thanks to the timely warning, the British-Canadian forces were able to repel them successfully.

June 25 – The Burning of Hampton, Virginia, takes place. A British raiding party led by Rear Admiral George Cockburn led an attack on the town of Hampton and burned it down. Despite fierce resistance from the local militia, the battle ended with a British victory.

August 10 – The Battle of St. Michaels takes place. This was another expedition led by Admiral Cockburn, but this one resulted in an American victory.

August 30 –The Fort Mims massacre takes place in Alabama. Part of the Creek War, an army of Red Sticks, led by Chief Red Eagle and Peter McQueen, massacred the inhabitants of Fort Mims, leading to strong anti-Native American sentiment among the American public.

September 10 – The Battle of Lake Erie takes place. This is also considered the largest and most significant naval conflict in the War of 1812, with the Americans scoring a major victory.

October 5 – The Battle of the Thames. Tecumseh is killed, signaling the end of Tecumseh's War.

October 26 – The Battle of the Chateauguay takes place. Despite having superior numbers, the American forces were untrained and inexperienced, allowing the Lower Canadian British and Native American forces to counter them successfully.

November 3 – The Battle of Tallushatchee takes place. Part of the Creek War, this battle was a decisive victory for the American forces under John Coffee. This skirmish was part of Andrew Jackson's campaign to subdue the Red Sticks.

November 9 – The Battle of Talladega takes place. Like the Battle of Tallushatchee, it resulted in another American victory under Andrew Jackson himself. Despite an overwhelming victory, Jackson's forces were broken apart over the course of the next month.

November 11 – The Battle of Crysler's Farm takes place. Like the Battle of the Chateauguay, the British-Canadian forces won an overwhelming victory despite great odds once again.

November 29 – The Battle of Autossee takes place. This was a short and brutal skirmish, where approximately 200 Red Sticks were killed by the joint American and Creek forces led by General John Floyd. Both forces were evenly matched, with the American-Creek forces standing at 1,400, while the Red Stick forces stood at 1,500.

December 19 – The Capture of Fort Niagara takes place. An important victory for the British-Canadian forces, Gordon Drummond led the British to a strategic victory. Leading 560 regulars and militiamen, Drummond led a surprise attack that overwhelmed the fort's inhabitants over the course of a single night.

1814

January 22–24 – The Battles of Emuckfaw and Enotachopo Creek takes place. These were the first battles led by Andrew Jackson after reorganizing his forces in the early days of January. The battles resulted in a draw, causing Jackson to retreat to his encampment at Fort Rogers.

January 27 – The Battle of Calebee Creek takes place. General John Floyd successfully led the American forces against the hostile Red Sticks, driving them back.

March 27 – The Battle of Horseshoe Bend takes place. This battle effectively ended the Creek War and was one of its largest battles. All hostile Creek were killed in the battle since they refused to surrender.

March 30 – The Battle of Lacolle Mill takes place. Technically, this is the second Battle of Lacolle Mill, but the first one (which took place in 1812) is not taken into consideration by many historians due to its small size. The British-Canadian forces managed to push back the Americans, securing a victory.

April 13 – The Treaty of Fontainebleau is ratified. Napoleon had already abdicated the throne by this point, and this treaty exiled him to Elba, which is located off the coast of Tuscany. This treaty also allowed Great Britain to turn its focus to the war in America.

May 6 – The Battle of Fort Oswego takes place.

May 14–16 – The Raid on Port Dover takes place. Without orders, Lieutenant Colonel John Campbell and his men destroyed private homes and property. This event helped spur the British during the Burning of Washington.

July 3 –The Capture of Fort Erie takes place under US Major General Jacob Brown and Brigadier General Winfield Scott. The large American force moved toward Fort Erie with little damage and casualties, and the small British garrison surrendered very quickly after firing a few shots.

July 5 – The Battle of Chippawa occurs. Another stunning victory for the American army, this was the first battle in which the American infantry successfully stood their ground against the British regulars. Their victory in this battle greatly bolstered the confidence of their army.

July 22 – The Treaty of Greenville is signed. This treaty, signed between the Wyandots, Delawares, Shawanoese, Senecas, Miamies, and the US government, redefined the border of the Northwest Territory, giving the US settlers a foothold in the region in the coming decades.

July 25 – The Battle of Lundy's Lane, one of the most violent battles of the war, takes place. The Americans once again proved their newfound strength by defeating the British regulars. This battle finally convinced the British to take the American infantry as a serious threat.

August 4–September 21 – The Siege of Fort Erie takes place. This was one of the most protracted engagements in the War of 1812. Both sides suffered heavy casualties and losses—the British suffered nearly 1,550 casualties while the Americans suffered 1,075 casualties. The Americans managed to hold onto the fort in the end.

August 8 – Peace negotiations between the British and Americans begin in Europe. Both sides initially tried to stall the negotiations to give their armies a better chance to create better conditions under which to negotiate. When that didn't happen, peace was finalized by the end of the year.

August 9 – The Treaty of Fort Jackson is signed, ending the Creek War.

August 24 – The Battle of Bladensburg takes place. This is considered by many military historians as the "the greatest disgrace ever dealt to American arms." The American army suffered a humiliating defeat at the hands of the British forces led by Rear Admiral George Cockburn and Major General Robert Ross. This battle saw the fall of the US capital and the subsequent burning of Washington, D.C.

August 24 – The Burning of Washington, D.C.

August 29–September 2 – The Raid on Alexandria takes place. After capturing Fort Washington as a distraction for the British troops at the Battle of Bladensburg, Commodore James Gordon decided to capture Alexandria as it was a viable objective. But after three days of fighting, the Royal Navy made a tactical retreat.

September 6–11 – The Battle of Plattsburgh takes place. This five-day battle saw 11,000 British soldiers engaged with around 6,300 American soldiers. Naval warfare was also a big part of this battle, as an assortment of small ships and gunboats engaged with each other. After a day of fierce fighting, Prévost realized that even if Plattsburgh was captured, the British would be unable to maintain control as they didn't have control over Lake Champlain. As a result, he withdrew his forces, conceding defeat and realizing the impracticality of continuing the conflict.

September 12 – The Battle of North Point occurs. This battle saw the American forces repel a British amphibious attack. Despite having a numerical advantage over the Americans, the British forces were greatly demoralized by the death of Major General Ross early in the battle. His death paused the movement of the British forces, which gave the Americans time to reinforce their defenses in the region. As a result, the British abandoned their planned attack against Baltimore two days later.

September 14 – Francis Scott Key writes the poem, *Defence of Fort M'Henry*, which would later be set to a tune and become "The Star-Spangled Banner."

November 6 – The Battle of Malcolm's Mills takes place. This battle is the last skirmish to take place on Canadian soil in the War of 1812. A small American force of 800 led by Brigadier General Duncan McArthur was raiding Upper Canada when they routed a smaller British force of 550 near Malcolm's Mills. But shortly after this battle, the Americans retreated from Upper Canada permanently.

November 7–9 – The Battle of Pensacola occurs. One of Andrew Jackson's crowning achievements in the War of 1812, this battle saw the suppression of the Spanish and British military presence in Florida.

December 1 – The peace delegates resume their talks at Ghent. By this time, both sides realized that further fighting was fruitless and rushed to get a peace treaty signed.

December 24 – The Treaty of Ghent is signed by both the British and Americans. The official ratification of the treaty wouldn't be completed until February of the next year.

December 27 – The Treaty of Ghent is ratified by the British.

1815

January 9 – The Battle of New Orleans takes place. The Americans inflicted ten times the casualties they received to the attacking British forces. Major General Sir Edward Pakenham led the British forces and died in the battle. The British defeat is often attributed to poor planning and coordination.

February 17 – The United States Senate ratifies the Treaty of Ghent.

February 18 – The Treaty of Ghent is declared, thus ending the War of 1812.

February 20 – The USS *Constitution* attacks the HMS *Cyane* and HMS *Levant*. Although the war was over by this point, the men on board the ships were unaware.

April 6 – The "Dartmoor Massacre" at Dartmoor Prison in Devon, England, takes place. Seven American prisoners of war are killed, and 32 are wounded.

May 24 – The Battle of the Sink Hole takes place. This is unofficially the last military action of the War of 1812. A small band of Sauk engaged with the American forces in Missouri, unaware that the War of 1812 had already ended.

Chapter Four: The War of 1812- The Invasion of Canada

To have shrunk, under such circumstances, from manly resistance, would have been a degradation blasting our best and proudest hopes; it would have struck us from the high ranks where the virtuous struggles of our fathers had placed us, and have betrayed the magnificent legacy which we hold in trust for future generations. It would have acknowledged that on the element which forms three-fourths of the globe we inhabit, where all independent nations have equal and common rights, the American people were not an independent people, but colonists and vassals.

- President James Madison, November 1812

Stirring and provocative, the above passage was the expertly crafted rhetoric that President James Madison presented to the US Congress when proposing the bill for going to war against the British Empire. Despite being politically charged, there was much truth in President Madison's words. But the biggest mistake that the Madison administration made was thinking that they could take over the territory of Canada without a concrete plan. The decision was rushed, and the lack of motivation and drive among the upper echelon of the US Army was made apparent before the year had ended.

In a way, the War of 1812 was a humbling lesson for the American military. It showcased many of the organizational mistakes and flaws of the American forces, which were rectified after the war ended. The victory of the American Revolutionary War had instilled a false sense of superiority in the state militias, which made up the core of the US military backbone at that time. This all changed with the War of 1812. Until this war, Americans were skeptical of a standing army for two reasons—they considered it a threat to the sovereignty of individual states, and they deemed the expense of maintaining one was too excessive. But these state-based armed forces also came with some drawbacks. The loyalty-based nature of state militias made it impossible to train them effectively for a large-scale invasion since militia volunteers weren't too eager to leave their home and family. For many militiamen at that time, conquering another country wasn't even part of their job description, as the state militias were more of a defensive force instead of an offensive one. The level of training and discipline of individual militia units also varied from state to state—some states had well-organized militias with uniforms, while others were just civilians with guns who banded together. Higher-ranking officers were chosen out of popularity in these militias rather than merit, making their leadership problematic as well.

This lack of proper leadership was demonstrated best in the first year of the War of 1812, in which the US Army performed abysmally, although it did do well in a few instances. Communication also ended up being a huge factor for the defeats of the American forces. The lack of a standing army also meant that communication among different militia units was disorganized. Also, the road systems in North America and Canada were nowhere near as structured as they are today, further hampering coordinated troop movements. Given their numbers and resources, even if the factors of training and experience are taken off the board, the invasion of Canada could have been very easy if simultaneous attacks were made on Canada from multiple directions. But the biggest mistake made was inadequate leadership. Other than a few of the commanding officers, including the US Navy as a whole, Andrew Jackson, and William Henry Harrison, most of the commanders performed terribly in this war, despite being veterans of the American Revolutionary War.

When the war was declared, President Madison was faced with making the unfortunate choice of who would lead the Canadian invasion. The list of candidates did not inspire much confidence at all. On the one hand, he had inexperienced military officers who had a fairly high rank and courage but lacked the experience to take on such a strong foe as the British. On the other hand, he had experienced but decrepit commanders who were well past their prime with hands-on experience from the American Revolutionary War. What Madison and the War Hawks in Washington didn't account for was that the American Revolutionary War was a defensive war by nature. So, any veteran from that war wasn't suited to lead an offensive into enemy territory. Despite all of these factors, Madison decided to choose Brigadier General William Hull to lead the invasion into Canada. At the time of the invasion, Hull was 58 years old. While he was an accomplished soldier and leader, Hull was neither a good tactician nor strategist, a fact that helped make the first American invasion into Canada a failure. The American military decided to launch their invasion from Detroit, Michigan, with a string force of 7,000 militiamen.

Even with all these disadvantages stacked against them, the American forces still had a good chance of conquering Canada. Compared to them, the Canadian numbers were nothing, and they were spread thinly across the defensive line. But Isaac Brock counteracted this problem by allying the British and Canadian forces with the Native Americans. While he was actively looking for Native American allies, luck favored him, and he ended up in an alliance with Tecumseh. After the Battle of Tippecanoe, Tecumseh and his Shawnee followers were in a difficult position as well, as Tecumseh needed weapons and supplies. By allying themselves with the British, Tecumseh gained those much-needed items, while the British gained soldiers for their cause. Even though their alliance with the British had cost many Native American tribes a lot during the American Revolutionary War, they still allied themselves with the British once again out of necessity. It also helped that Brock made a good impression on Tecumseh and gained his approval as a warrior.

What helped win over the Native American tribes were Brock's early victories against the Americans. As soon as the war was declared, Captain Charles Roberts, who was posted on St. Joseph's Island, located in the northwestern part of Lake Huron, was ordered by Major General Brock to capture the American-held Fort Mackinac, which was located on Mackinac Island, near the Straits of Mackinac that connect Lake Michigan and Lake Huron. After weeks of preparations, the planned offensive was canceled and then authorized again over a course of ten days. Finally, on July 17th, Captain Roberts launched his attack on Fort Mackinac with a force of Native Americans, local fur traders, and British regulars, which numbered to more than 600 men.

The attack was the quintessential example of the phrase "like taking candy from a baby." Due to the ineffective American communication infrastructure, the inhabitants of Fort Mackinac weren't even aware that they were at war with the British. After landing on Mackinac Island, Captain Roberts and his men simply dragged their six-pound fieldpiece cannon onto a high point that faced the fort in the early hours of July 17th. After setting up their cannon, Captain Roberts sent an emissary to Lieutenant Porter Hanks, demanding an immediate surrender. This surprising turn of events, coupled with exaggerated reports of a Native American presence by the villagers who fled to the fort, convinced Hanks to cave into Roberts' demands and surrender. The aftermath was actually very civil, with little to no looting and the inhabitants being given one month's time to evacuate the premises. This victory was decisive in breaking American morale because soon afterward, Brigadier General William Hull stopped his march toward Canada and retreated back to the safe confines of Detroit.

While Hull was busy retreating with plans to attack Fort Amherstburg, the British-Canadian alliance was pushing forward with their victory at Mackinac Island to recruit more allies. After the victory at Fort Mackinac, the next major British victory came at the Battle of Brownstone, which took place on August 5th, 1812. This time, the Native Americans engaged without British assistance, although they were encouraged to do so by the British, against Major Thomas Van Horne, who was a part of Brigadier General Hull's forces. Major Horne was sent by Brigadier General Hull to River Raisin near Brownstown to pick up supplies and cattle for Fort Detroit. Despite having a fairly large force of 200 men, the American forces lost to the mere force of 25 men that were led by Tecumseh, Chief Daimee of the Chickamauga, and Chief Roundhead of the Wyandot tribe. This happened because the militia was untrained; when Van Horne called for a retreat, the majority of the men panicked and scattered. The Native American forces killed eighteen men and wounded twelve others. Seventy US soldiers were missing after this conflict, although many of them returned to Detroit in the following days.

After the news of this defeat reached Brigadier General Hull, he doubled down on the speed of his retreat while leaving Lieutenant Colonel James Miller with around 600 men to act as a standing force in Canada to retrieve the supplies Van Horne failed to capture. Hull also abandoned his plans to lay siege to Fort Amherstburg, but British Major General Brock was not aware of this. To strengthen the morale of the Canadian public and military forces, Brock had decided to move to Fort Amherstburg himself to oversee its defenses. In his absence, Major Adam Muir was left in charge of the defenses for Upper Canada. Unfortunately for Lieutenant Colonel Miller, he ran straight into Major Muir's force of 205 men near the

Wyandot village of Maguaga, located in modern-day Michigan, when he attempted to retrieve the intended supplies for Hull on August 9th. Despite having an advantage in numbers, Miller failed to win this skirmish due to being incapable of coordinating his men.

Many historians consider the Battle of Maguaga as a comedy of errors in US military history. When the attack began, the British forces ended up shooting at their Potawatomi allies instead of the Americans, giving away their position and losing the element of surprise. But then Miller made the mistake of ordering the bugle to be sounded, which sent the British forces into a timely retreat, as the bugle was used by the light infantry in the British Army. When the bugle was sounded, some of Muir's men took it as an order to retreat, and they fell back while the American forces charged into the location where they had been gathered just moments ago. This resulted in total confusion for Miller's forces, as they believed they had won when they were suddenly attacked by Muir's men, who had been rallied by their commander. The surprise attack left eighteen Americans dead and many more wounded; Muir had far fewer casualties. Miller's nerve was so broken by this skirmish that he set up camp, refusing to either retrieve the supplies or return to Fort Detroit, despite receiving repeated orders from Brigadier General Hull. Major Muir, on the other hand, sailed his forces immediately after this skirmish to travel to Fort Amherstburg.

Just a few days after this, the Siege of Fort Detroit took place. Brock and Tecumseh acted with a speed that astonished the American army, which had already been demoralized by Brock's and Tecumseh's previous attacks. Within just days of meeting each other in early August 1812, the British and the Native American forces joined together for an attack on Fort Detroit. The Siege of Fort Detroit took place on August 15th, 1812, and ended a day later with only two wounded on the British side. Outnumbered and facing a fortified city that could withstand an attack for months, Brock and Tecumseh followed a plan that relied more on cunning and tactics rather than numbers and brute strength. They had around 1,330

Native American warriors, British regulars, and militiamen at their disposal, while Brigadier General Hull had nearly 2,200 men, more than enough to put up a solid defense. However, Brigadier General Hull wasn't even prepared for attacking Canada, let alone face an attack from them. Added to that was his inordinate fear of the savagery of the Native Americans, whom he considered to be hellish. Brock and Tecumseh's main tactic for the Siege of Fort Detroit was fooling the American army into thinking that they were facing a large organized force instead of the paltry numbers they had. Brock inventively dressed his militia troops in surplus British military uniforms. As a result, the Americans were fooled into believing that the British troops were all trained veterans. Tecumseh wasn't keen on doing this ploy subtlety, though—he marched his warriors thrice around the fort to convince the Americans that the Native Americans also had superior numbers as well. After this trick, the British fired a cannon shot at Fort Detroit that killed seven men, including the aforementioned Lieutenant Porter Hanks of the Fort Mackinac disaster. The combined cunning of both these leaders worked perfectly, as the morale of Hull's men and Hull himself was crippled beyond repair. After the cannon fire, Hull immediately asked for a three-day ceasefire to which Brock replied that if Hull didn't surrender in three hours, he would level the fort. The threat worked—Hull surrendered within minutes of receiving this message, ending the first Canadian invasion in disgrace and disaster.

On a separate note, on the same day the Siege of Fort Detroit started, another important battle also took place, which is known as the Battle of Fort Dearborn (also known as the Fort Dearborn massacre). A short and decisive battle that only lasted about fifteen minutes, the event is often considered to be more of a massacre due to the large number of soldiers and civilians killed in the battle. The Potawatomi tribe, led by Chief Blackbird, was the force behind this attack, with their numbers being between 400 and 500 men. The Americans in Fort Dearborn, a fort which is near present-day Chicago, Illinois, only numbered to 66; there were also 27 civilians present. The dispute seemed to have risen over a Captain William Wells not following through on his promises. He had proposed to the Potawatomi tribe through Miami delegates that in exchange for escorting the inhabitants of the fort to Fort Wayne, he would pay them well and leave surplus alcohol and weapon supplies for the Potawatomi. But Wells reneged on his word, as he ordered the promised provisions to be destroyed, fearing that the Native Americans would only cause mischief if these items were left in their hands. This strained relationships between the Americans and the young men of the Potawatomi, who were angered by Wells' decision. So, on the day the garrison set out for Fort Wayne, they were ambushed on the way by the Potawatomi and mercilessly slaughtered. While fifteen Potawatomi died, 38 soldiers and 14 civilians were killed; the rest of the people heading for Fort Wayne were captured. This unfortunate incident convinced many American politicians and top military brass to focus fanatically on the Native American removal policy that became a huge issue throughout the 19th century.

On September 21st, 1812, a short skirmish took place at the British outpost of Gananoque, which was located near the St. Lawrence River. More of a raid than a full-scale attack, the New York militia was looking to resupply their ammunition reserves after failing to procure any properly after the attack on Sacket's Harbor. This skirmish ended in a positive note for the American army, as they successfully managed to accomplish their objectives. The New York militia, led by Captain Benjamin Forsyth, surprised the British militia and subjugated them quickly. The British suffered eight deaths, with eight more taken as prisoners, including the wife of Joel Stone, the founder and commander of Gananoque. While the raid turned out to be a success for the Americans, Canadian defenses were strengthened after the attack.

Even though the first invasion of Canada ended in total disaster, the American army bounced back with marvelous resilience. The second invasion of Canada started in October of the same year, 1812, after

US troops gathered at Lewiston. Lewiston was situated just opposite to the quant Canadian town called Queenston, which was soon to become the first scene of conflict in this second wave of attacks. The American forces were led by Stephen Van Rensselaer this time around, but in a way, his command was worse than Brigadier General William Hull. Though Van Rensselaer was an able administrator and politician, he had zero military experience. On the other hand, the British had their hero in Isaac Brock, who had successfully fended off the first American invasion. As soon as Brock heard of the American forces gathering at Lewistown, he immediately set sail for Queenston.

The Battle of Queenston Heights was essentially the battle for Upper Canada. Brock was well aware that if the Americans broke through Queenston, then it would be as good as conquering the entirety of Upper Canada since Brock had focused most of the British defenses in Lower Canada. On October 13th, 1812, the US troops mobilized from Lewistown and started crossing the Niagara River for the second invasion of Canada. The Americans had a total number of 3,550 troops, with the bulk of this number being militiamen. Rensselaer decided to employ his forces in a rather straightforward manner by swarming the enemy numbers head-on. The British, on the other hand, had only managed to muster 1,300 soldiers, which included trained regulars, local militiamen, and Native Americans. This battle could have been an easy victory for the Americans except for one fact—the American army had to cross the Niagara River first. Instead of crossing the river in big boats, they used thirteen smaller boats to transfer the troops in turns. This ended up being their undoing at the Battle of Queenston Heights. After the first wave of American troops landed, they actually made good tactical decisions by overtaking the bluff known as Queenston Heights, gaining the tactical advantage of higher ground. The British forces were pinned down, and in a desperate charge to break through the enemy lines, Major General Isaac Brock lost his life. After he was shot down, the fighting grew fiercer, as Tecumseh's warriors, who had been suspiciously quiet during the whole affair, made their move. The Native Americans were extremely good at guerilla warfare, which spelled doom for the American militia.

While the British kept the Americans busy on the frontlines, the Native American warriors stealthily flanked the British and made their way up Queenston Heights. Their style of warfare was using natural elements as cover to reach the enemy so that they would be within melee range before launching an attack. Once they got into close quarters, the Native Americans ambushed the American army from behind, overwhelming them within a short period of time. The sound of the dying men on the Canadian side of the river, along with the wild Native American war cries, crushed the spirit of the American forces who had yet to cross the river. They were stalled long enough for British Major General Roger Sheaffe to arrive and take command of the situation. Once the Americans launched their second assault, the British forces under Sheaffe countered back. Following this counterattack, Brigadier General William Wadsworth, who was leading the American troops at Queenston Heights, surrendered to the Canadian forces with 500 of his men. This was the conclusion of the second American invasion of Canada. Though the second invasion was staved off, the Americans would make one more attempt at invading Canada. After the Battle of Queenston Heights, Stephen Van Rensselaer immediately resigned from his position, only to be succeeded by Brigadier General Alexander Smyth, who drove the campaign in a worse direction.

After the failure of his predecessor, Smyth decided to make reparations the following month at the Battle of Frenchman's Creek. Incidentally, the Battle of Wild Cat Creek also took place on the same day (a battle that will be covered in a later chapter). On November 22nd, 1812, Smyth made another attempt to cross into Canada by crossing the Niagara River from Frenchman's Creek. Just like the Battle of Queenston Heights, the purpose of this battle was to set up a launching point for American troops in the forthcoming Canadian invasion. Learning from Van Rensselaer's mistake at

Queenston Heights, Smyth decided to split his force into three bodies. A small company of 220 and 200 men led by Captain William King and Lieutenant Colonel Charles Boerstler, respectively, would cross the Niagara beforehand and put pressure on the British defenses from two sides while Smyth himself would lead the main body from the center once the enemy was occupied. The two forces were nearly matched with the British troops, as they numbered to around 650 and the American troops numbered about 770.

On pen and paper, this sounds like a very solid plan, but unexpected circumstances can derail the best-laid schemes. Firstly, the lack of coordination in King's detachment led to only a small portion of troops landing at Red House, which was his intended target. Even though he managed to accomplish his objectives of disabling the British cannons and artillery, it ultimately didn't impact the battle. King split his detachment into two smaller forces, giving command of the other force to Lieutenant Samuel Angus, who failed to coordinate with him properly. Lieutenant Colonel Boerstler's attack also met the same fate due to lack of coordination, but he successfully managed to retreat, whereas King failed to do so. As a result, Smyth's plans to pin down the British forces ended up in smoke. The British forces, on the other hand, coordinated properly and held their positions with great tenacity and eventually were joined by reinforcements, bolstering their numbers. When dawn broke the next day, King, who was trapped on the Canadian side of the Niagara, was forced to surrender. Smyth, however, had received news that King had succeeded in his mission but not what happened afterward. As a result, Smyth blindly ordered his forces, led by Colonel William Winder, to land at Frenchman's Creek. Once there, they found Lieutenant Colonel Cecil Bisshopp and 300 British regulars waiting for them with their guns at the ready. Finding themselves in a precarious position, the Americans immediately retreated. Smyth tried to take over Frenchman's Creek a second time on November 31st, 1812, but that attack also ended in failure. After this disastrous performance, Smyth took a leave to visit his family in Virginia and wasn't heard of again until after the war, which was when he started practicing law.

Although the British-Canadian-Native American forces were performing admirably in the battles against the Americans, Isaac Brock's death had been a huge blow to the British-Canadian forces. So much so, that after his death, the effectiveness of the Canadian forces was almost reduced in half. When compared to the success of his predecessor, George Prévost fell surprisingly short. So, in a way, it was fortunate for the Canadian forces that the third American invasion of Canada never took off properly. Major General Henry Dearborn, also derisively called "Granny Dearborn," was the man who would go on to lead the third American invasion of Canada. Old, slow, and very conservative, Dearborn had neither the energy nor the morale required to lead such an expedition. The first two invasions had already ended in total failure, but Dearborn had the support of some of the best strategists of the US Army. He also managed to stay in the fight the longest and even managed to survive the end of the war without any damage to his reputation. While his performance in the war was poor, Hull and Van Rensselaer's defeats also left him void of any means to engage with the British forces properly since he wasn't allowed any time to conscript troops from New England, which became the only state that didn't raise or fund any troops in the War of 1812. While Hull was entrenched in Detroit, Dearborn was planning to attack Montreal, Kingston, Fort Niagara, and Amherstburg simultaneously. His plans failed for two reasons: lack of troops and the slow speed of his troops. His only military successes in the War of 1812 were the Battle of York and the Siege of Fort George, which both occurred in 1813. In July 1813, Major General Dearborn was recalled from frontline duty and served the rest of the war in an administrative capacity.

On April 27th, 1813, full-scale land warfare commenced once again with the Battle of York, signaling the third invasion of Canada under Henry Dearborn. York, which is now present-day Toronto, was the stage for this American victory. Unlike the previous American military initiatives, this campaign was well planned and well thought out. The US Army didn't only use ground troops for this battle; they also successfully used their naval forces. Commodore Isaac Chauncey led the American naval forces in this battle, while the infantry was led by Brigadier General Zebulon Pike, whose forces were mostly trained regulars of the US Army. On the other hand, the British were woefully underprepared and outnumbered in this battle, which was out of the norm. Major General Roger Sheaffe, who had previously oversaw the victory at the Battle of Queenston Heights, was in charge of York when the American attack happened. He had gone there for administrative purposes, and the command was thrust on him suddenly, resulting in poor defense and scouting. The town was also low on supplies, which was already a big problem when the Americans attacked in full force. The American force had 1,700 soldiers and 14 naval vessels with them, while the British force stood at 600, half of them militiamen. There was also between forty to fifty Ojibway present on the British side. The defenders tried their best to engage with the enemy, but the constant artillery bombardment from the American gunboats derailed their plans, forcing them to fall back. The British forces made their last stand at the western blockhouse of York before surrendering. The British-Canadian-Native American forces had 82 deaths on their side, while the Americans had 55, including Brigadier General Zebulon Pike. Despite receiving strict orders not to destroy civilian property, the American soldiers set about plundering and burning the city on April 28th. The commanders were so appalled by their men's actions that they left the area as soon as possible. Due to the British surrendering, the town was not completely destroyed and would see two more American excursions in the months of July and August the same year. Although this battle was a tactical victory for the Americans, it wasn't as important as an objective as Kingston, which was where the British vessels were based. The original plan was to attack Kingston and then York, but the plan had been changed since Major

General Dearborn had falsely heard that there were far too many numbers to deal with at Kingston.

A month later, on May 27th, 1813, the US Army saw another victory with the Battle of Fort George. This was the first major offensive in Canada in six months after the second invasion of Canada was stalled at the Battle of Queenston Heights. Also, this was the last and final wave of the American invasion of Canada. Like in the Battle of York, the US forces in the Battle of Fort George were a combination of land and naval troops. They also had overwhelming numbers—4,000 infantrymen, 12 gunboats, and one brig-of-war. Facing those overwhelming odds were only 1,000 British infantry, 300 militia, and 50 Native Americans, with a few artillery pieces. Brigadier General John Vincent, who was in charge of the British troops in the Niagara Peninsula at that time, was at a total loss on what to do—the troops he had weren't enough to lay down a proper defense for the fort since he didn't know from which side the Americans would attack. Taking the American strategy from the Battle of York into consideration, Vincent safely assumed that there would be a two-pronged attack, and he split his forces into defensive positions accordingly. But despite the accuracy of his assumption, his forces were simply overwhelmed by the superior US numbers and the constant bombardment of the American navy. The battle began on May 25th, and the first wave of American infantry who landed at Fort George was beaten back within minutes and almost cost the life of their commander, Colonel Winfield Scott. But the steady barrage of American artillery gradually pushed the British forces back, allowing the subsequent landings of the American infantry to be successful. Scott gave chase to Vincent's retreating forces but was ordered to stop because Major General Morgan Lewis, his superior officer, felt that Vincent was leading them into a trap. Despite the scale of the battle, the casualties on both sides weren't as horrific as many of the previous battles of the north had been. The American army tallied a total death count of 41, while the British deaths are estimated to be between around 60 to a little over 100. After the fall of Fort George, the entirety of Upper Canada was under American control for a few months. This victory also marked the rise of Oliver Hazard Perry, the hero of the Battle of Lake Erie that occurred the same year (this battle is talked about in more detail in the chapter on naval battles).

The British-Canadian forces wouldn't take this defeat lying down and made their comeback in the Battle of Stoney Creek, but despite their victory, the Americans maintained control of Fort George until the end of the year. On June 6th, 1813, a British-Canadian force of 700 men led by Brigadier General John Vincent and Lieutenant Colonel John Harvey ambushed the American camp at Stoney Creek at night. The expedition was originally meant to be a scouting mission, but Harvey couldn't resist the temptation of attacking the American forces when they were completely off guard. Harvey had obtained the password for crossing the American lines (how he came upon it is unclear, though), and using this advantage, he stealthily led his large force near the American camp without facing any challenges. Once the British Army had closed in, they suddenly lost the element of surprise when a few overeager militiamen started cheering for their forces. The Americans were wary of such an attack since the Battle of Frenchtown and quickly countered back. But in their rush, they left their artillery unit exposed, which the British soldiers quickly brought down. Once their artillery was down, the American soldiers were thrown into complete chaos and were unable to regroup. Another reason why the American army was in total disarray was that, in an ironic turn of events, the American commanders ended up walking into the British lines and were captured. After this battle, the movements of American troops were restricted to Fort George and the borders of the Niagara River.

In response to this attack at Stoney Creek, the American army led an expedition from Fort George to Beaver Dams on June 24th, 1813, to regain some control in Upper Canada. The expedition ended in failure when the American forces were ambushed by Native American warriors during their march toward Beaver Dams. The

American force was fairly large, with 600 regular infantrymen, while the Kahnawake had 300 warriors participating in this skirmish. There were also 100 Mohawk warriors and fifty British regulars, but the Kahnawake made up the bulk of the force. British Lieutenant James FitzGibbon was in charge of the Beaver Dams outpost and later joined the Native American forces to beat back the American force in the Battle of Beaver Dams. The initial Native American ambush greatly demoralized the American troops since their commander, Colonel Charles Boerstler, was wounded in it. Thankfully, Lieutenant FitzGibbon arrived in time to offer a truce, which the Americans accepted. By doing this, Lieutenant FitzGibbon probably avoided another major Native American massacre in the War of 1812.

The next battle to take place on Canadian soil in the War of 1812 was the Battle of Crysler's Farm. Taking place on November 11th, 1813, this battle was a major turning point for the Canadians, as it ended the American victory streak following the consecutive victories at York, Fort George, and Lake Erie. Another reason this battle is so important is that this was the largest assembly of American forces in the War of 1812, and yet they were defeated by an army a fraction of their size. The British numbers were comparatively laughable, comprising of only 900 regulars and militia; the Americans had close to 8,000 regulars. Yet despite this overwhelming disparity, the American forces sustained more casualties and damage than the British. The American army was led by Major General James Wilkinson, Brigadier General John Parker Boyd, and Brigadier General Leonard Covington. On the other side, the British had Lieutenant Colonel Joseph W. Morrison and Commander William Mulcaster to lead them. The Americans' intended target was the Canadian city of Montreal, which would help to greatly eliminate British influence.

Before the battle took place, it is important to take into consideration the events that precipitated it. On October 17th, 1813, Major General James Wilkinson sailed out of Sacket's Harbor, New York, with his

8,000 troops. The pace of the American ships was very slow, and it took them 21 days to reach their destination of the St. Lawrence River before Wilkinson finally held a council of war on November 9th. The British forces in Canada had received reports of Wilkinson's movement and had prepared themselves for an attack on Kingston, their main base of operations. The assumption was made based on the fact that the primary American military goal in Canada was to capture Kingston, a goal that had been in place since the beginning of the War of 1812 (in fact, Kingston was going to be the original goal this time around as well, except Commodore Isaac Chauncey did not want to risk his men in pitched battle against the well-fortified base of Kingston). By the time the British realized that the Americans were making a move for Montreal instead of Kingston, they didn't have enough time to scrape together a large force. Under urgent orders from Governor General George Prévost, Lieutenant Colonel Joseph Morrison led the British charge to interrupt the American invasion with a meager force of 650 men. Carefully evading the American ships led by Brigadier General Boyd, who had arrived to assist Wilkinson's troops, the British-Canadian forces successfully landed on Prescott on November 9th, and they made their way to just outside Crysler's Farm on November 10th, the day before the battle.

The British-Canadian forces led their charge against the American army in the early hours of November 11th, 1813. The weather was bad, as it was cold and raining, but British Lieutenant Colonel Morrison's troops braved the assault, attacking the American army from two points near Cook's Point, a location near the American camp where their ships were docked. The Americans initially led a successful counterattack under the command of Colonel Eleazer Wheelock Ripley, who pushed the British forces a mile into their own lines. But the American forces made the mistake of taking a rest and waiting for reinforcements to arrive before advancing. When they started moving again, they were ambushed from all sides by British regulars, who forced them to fall back. This allowed the

British to gain control of the battlefield again and proceed with their offense. The attack was highly effective, and within a couple of hours, the American army was forced into a retreat due to running out of ammunition. The British forces suffered heavy losses while advancing toward the American position, which Brigadier General Boyd, who was in command of the battle, failed to take advantage of. The Americans retreated into their boats and left the region after taking a lot of damage—102 were dead, 120 were taken as prisoners, and another 237 were wounded within the short space of few hours. The British, on the other hand, had 31 dead and 148 wounded. Even though the Americans had brought an overwhelming force with them, like in their previous victories in Canada, what they failed to do was deploy all of them—it is estimated that only a quarter of the 8,000 soldiers that had landed fought in the Battle of Crysler's Farm.

The Battle of Crysler's Farm seemed to turn the tables of fortune once again for the Americans, as they suffered another major defeat in the Capture of Fort Niagara, which took place on American soil on December 19th. The huge number of troops deployed in the invasion of Montreal had left most of the major US strategic positions with exposed defenses. There weren't many troops left after that attack to defend these military positions, which Lieutenant General Gordon Drummond took full advantage of. Despite winning the Battle of Crysler's Farm, the British, especially Major General Francis de Rottenburg, the British lieutenant governor of Upper Canada, were convinced the Americans would continue with their expedition toward Montreal, and de Rottenburg ordered all available troops to retreat to Burlington Heights, which was located close to Toronto. However, before de Rottenburg could continue his plans with enforcing Kingston, he was replaced by Lieutenant General Drummond. Drummond knew the Americans had been defeated in their plans to take Montreal, so instead of retreating according to his predecessor's orders, he decided to make a move for Fort George. The move was perfectly timed since the Americans had hastily retreated from Fort George to Fort Niagara, as they didn't have the troops to hold both positions at once. While making the retreat, the Americans also burned down the town of Newark, which was adjacent to Fort George, to slow down the British forces. Normally, this wouldn't have been an issue since civilians were usually given time and compensation for the damage to their property if a town or settlement was destroyed for strategic purposes. But the Americans burned Newark within a matter of two hours, leaving the occupants helpless and without aid in the harsh winter. The outrage of this action would be used by the British to justify similar actions on their end in future events of the War of 1812.

After taking over Fort George, General Drummond sent a small military expedition consisting of 562 men under the command of Colonel John Murray to capture Fort Niagara. The British force again took advantage of subterfuge and slowly made their way toward Fort Niagara. They captured the outpost of Youngstown on their way and took some prisoners. One of the prisoners gave the British colonel the password for the American checkpoints, which gave them an overwhelming advantage once again. A couple of British artillery soldiers and officers marched forward to the entrance of Fort Niagara and confused the guards at the checkpoint long enough to allow the rest of their forces into the fort. From there on, the British took over the fort quite easily, meeting little resistance except for the south redoubt of the fort where some of the defenders had barricaded themselves. After refusing to give themselves up, despite warnings from the British, British troops broke into the building and killed all of the men. The British kept control of the fort until the end of the War of 1812. This also marked the end of all major land battles in 1813.

Following the defeat at Crysler's Farm, the American forces under Major General Wilkinson took shelter in French Mills, New York, which was just across the Canadian border. Though the British had feared that Wilkinson would soon be leading a counterattack, they had nothing to fear. The men on the American side were sick, supplies were low, and the weather was really bad. The sickness among the men spread to such a degree that Secretary of War John Armstrong ordered Wilkinson to divide his troops and move them to Burlington, Vermont, before making any other moves. After the move had been made, Wilkinson started planning some offensives against the British to reclaim his reputation, but most of them were unfeasible plans. Finally, he decided on attacking Lacolle Mill, located along the Lacolle River.

Leading 4,000 troops, Wilkinson first decided to occupy Odelltown, which he was unable to do due to the thick snow that was hindering troop movements. Despite these odds, Wilkinson decided to launch his attack on Lacolle Mill on the morning of March 30th, 1814, and ordered his artillery units to fire their cannons at the British position. The British, who only had 500 men, fired back with Congreve rockets, which were totally new to the American army and frightened them. These rockets were highly inaccurate, but they had a large area of impact, which balanced out its inaccuracy. With these new pieces of artillery, the defending forces caused significant casualties on the American side without major damage to their side. To make matters worse, the grenadier and light infantry units that Wilkinson had reserved for a surprise attack once the main attack was underway also failed and was repelled. Hearing the cannon shots, a company of Canadian Voltigeurs, which was a light infantry unit, and the Canadian Fencibles, which was a grenadier unit, who were nearby rushed toward the source of fire to defend Lacolle Mill. Instead of using land terrain like the Americans, the Canadian reinforcements waded through the Lacolle River, flanked the Americans, and attacked them from behind, causing further chaos and confusion among the American ranks. And to top off Wilkinson's bad luck, Commander Daniel Pring of the Royal Navy also came to the rescue with some of his gunboats, which started bombarding the American position with artillery fire. The Americans had no means to fire back and suddenly found themselves between a rock and a hard place, despite their overwhelming numbers. By the end of the day, Wilkinson again ordered a retreat, this time to

Plattsburgh. Upon reaching Plattsburgh, he was relieved of his duties and court-martialed, ending his service in the War of 1812.

Since taking over Fort George and Fort Niagara at the end of 1813, Lieutenant General Gordon Drummond kept a low profile in the early months of 1814 until he planned an attack on Fort Oswego with Commodore Sir James Yeo. Initially, the two men planned to attack Sacket's Harbor, but after careful reconsideration, they decided to attack Fort Oswego first since it was a strategic supply point for the American forces. Their target was to proceed to Sacket's Harbor after capturing Fort Oswego with the intention of capturing the guns that were at Sacket's Harbor. On May 3rd, Yeo set out from Kingston with 8 warships, 200 sailors, 400 marines, and 550 soldiers toward Fort Oswego. Yeo's forces reached Fort Oswego by midday but had trouble landing due to the weather. American Major George Mitchell of the 3rd Artillery led the defenses in Fort Oswego, who had 242 regulars stationed, along with 200 militiamen. The British frigates, the HMS *Prince Regent* and *Princess Charlotte*, starting firing on the fort under Yeo's command since his troops couldn't land. Eventually, they managed to land, and despite being under heavy fire from the fort, the British forces charged toward the fort and, after some time, forced the Americans to surrender, winning a decisive victory. In the aftermath of the battle, the British forces captured significant supplies from the fort as well as a few schooners. But Yeo soon figured out that his main objectives, the guns, were already en route to Sacket's Harbor. In order to prevent them from reaching their destination, Yeo ordered a blockade, which was broken by the Americans, allowing the guns to reach their destination safely. In the end, this battle turned out to be ineffective since the Americans were able to maintain control in Lake Ontario until the end of the War of 1812.

It wasn't until the middle of the War of 1812 that the American soldiers finally stood toe to toe with the British Army. The first two years were filled with devastating losses for the Americans due to multiple factors, but the biggest reason was the lack of trained soldiers. The Battle of Chippawa and the Battle of Lundy's Lane were both fought in the month of July 1814. On July 5th, 1814, 3,564 trained US soldiers engaged with the Canadian forces in Chippawa, Upper Canada. Led by Major General Jacob Brown, Brigadier General Winfield Scott, and Brigadier General Peter Porter, this was a major victory for the American troops after the constant string of defeats in the early months of 1814. The British forces, numbering 2,000, were led by Major General Phineas Riall, who was comparatively new to the battlefield. Riall took the offensive first and started firing at the American camp early on the morning on July 5th. In a stroke of luck, the British even managed to capture Winfield Scott in this early ambush while he was having breakfast. Undeterred by Scott's capture, Captain Nathaniel Towson's company started firing his cannons toward the British position, destroying ammunition and vital artillery positions. The British were shocked; the American forces had pushed back in the past but only in advantageous situations. This time, they stood unfazed by the British attack and countered in an organized manner, surprising Riall, who was expecting an attack force made up of untrained militia. The British forces were further weakened due to poor formation orders by Riall, which forced the British forces to take a lot of casualties. After almost half an hour of fighting, the British forces retreated, giving the Americans a decisive victory. Scott was also rescued by the American forces at the end of the battle. Following this battle, the Americans pushed through the Canadian lines, forcing the British to fall back to Fort George, and they finally took over Kingston after two and a half years of effort.

Twenty days after the Battle of Chippawa, the Battle of Lundy's Lane took place. Though the Americans won an overwhelming victory at the Battle of Chippawa, the Battle of Lundy's Lane ended up in a strategic draw, despite the excellent performance by the American troops. According to many historians, this was also the bloodiest and most violent battle of the War of 1812. Both sides also received reinforcements during the day, which changed the tides of the battle. US Major General Jacob Brown launched his attack on the British lines with 1,000 men and three guns along the Niagara River, later receiving an additional 1,500 men and six guns as support. The British forces, led by Lieutenant General Gordon Drummond, started with 1,800 men and five guns, with 1,700 men and three additional guns coming in as reinforcement later. After a few hours of intense fighting, the British forces were pushed back, but the fighting went on throughout the day. By the time evening had settled in, it was the Americans who were now on the defensive due to the strong British defense line, which they maintained after their initial retreat. But a problem for the British became apparent once the Americans captured all of their artillery pieces. To turn the situation around, Lieutenant General Drummond led two disorganized counterattacks to break through the US ranks and get back their artillery, which failed but caused a lot of damage nonetheless. By nightfall, both sides were broken down and could barely stand. Seeing the condition of his troops, US Major General Brown ordered a retreat for the American forces to Fort Erie, which allowed the British to fall back as well. The only good thing that came out of this battle for the Canadians was that the British finally regained control of Kingston once more. The casualties on both sides were high. The British dead stood at 84, while the American soldiers had almost double that number, numbering 174 dead. Both sides had almost an equal number of wounded soldiers, 559 and 572 soldiers, respectively.

The following month saw the American forces victorious at the Siege of Fort Erie, which was also the last British offensive in the north in the War of 1812. After the Battle of Lundy's Lane, the American forces that took part in the battle retreated to Fort Erie under Brigadier General Eleazer Ripley since Major General Jacob Brown was wounded in the previous battle. The British-Canadian forces assembled their largest force in the War of 1812, which numbered to 4,800, led by Lieutenant General Drummond. The initial speed of General Drummond's forces was very slow, which allowed the Americans at Fort Erie to bolster their defenses well.

The siege started on August 4th, 1814, but on the day before, Drummond had sent a small expedition across the Niagara to destroy American supplies and ammunitions. The attack was led by Lieutenant Colonel John Tucker and ultimately ended in failure. When Tucker and his men arrived, they found the bridge over Conjocta Creek destroyed and guarded by US troops, who fired at them. Tucker and his men were forced to retreat, suffering eleven deaths and seventeen wounded.

It took Lieutenant General Drummond ten days to prepare for the siege while the Americans watched from the other side of the Niagara. Three American schooners, the USS *Ohio*, *Porcupine*, and *Somers*, tried to disrupt the British preparations by peppering them with artillery; *Ohio* and *Somers* were captured. The USS *Porcupine* managed to get away but, in doing so, accidentally fired upon the US artillery on the shore.

On August 13th, Lieutenant General Drummond began his attack on Fort Erie. The first two days were spent trying to wear down the fort's defenses with cannon fire, which ended up being ineffective. In response to this, Drummond employed a night raid on Fort Erie. The plan was simple. Two thousand men would be divided into two companies of 1,300 and 700 men, led by Lieutenant Colonel Victor Fischer and Colonel Hercules Scott, respectively. Fischer would outflank the southern defenses, while Scott would attack the northern end. Lieutenant Colonel William Drummond would attack the fort with 360 men once the other assaults were underway. Fischer and Scott fought valiantly with no results. The defenses on both sides of the fort were solid, and both men were forced to retreat after attempting to lead their assault. William Drummond, on the other hand, fared much better. The strategy didn't go exactly as planned, but he unintentionally thinned down the American defenses in front of the fort as they were called to respond to Fischer's and Scott's attacks. After two unsuccessful charges, Drummond's forces managed to capture one of the American cannons inside the fort, which turned the tide of the battle. Using the captured cannon proved to be disastrous, as after a few shots, the cannon exploded, instantly killing between 150 and 250 men. Almost half of Drummond's squad was wiped out, but they managed to force the Americans to retreat.

After capturing the fort, it was the Americans who then carried out multiple assaults to recapture the fort with no effect except for the last one. During this whole time, Lieutenant General Gordon Drummond had a difficult time—he had to overlook the fort's defenses while lacking supplies and medicine for his men who were becoming sick. After multiple unsuccessful attempts, the American army finally demolished the fort on September 17th, 1814. US Brigadier General Peter Porter led the attack with 1,600 militia and employed shock tactics to get through the enemy defenses, taking over the British line of defense rapidly. Following this defeat, Gordon Drummond retreated to Fort George with the remaining 2,000 troops he had on September 21st.

In between the interim of the Siege of Fort Erie and its destruction, another monumental large-scale battle took place called the Battle of Bladensburg, which was located less than nine miles from Washington, D.C. Also known as the "the greatest disgrace ever dealt to American arms," this battle was graced with the presence of President James Madison himself, as well as African American soldiers. After Napoleon had abdicated his throne, President Madison and his Cabinet grew worried that the British would finally get serious about the war in America. The US Cabinet knew that so far the only reason the Americans had a fighting chance was because Britain was occupied with the Napoleonic Wars. After much discussion between President Madison and Secretary of War John Armstrong, they assumed that the British would be more interested in attacking Baltimore than Washington, D.C., the capital of America. But their assumption was proven wrong when the British attacked both Baltimore and Washington, D.C., burning down the latter city.

The Battle of Bladensburg was spread out over a large geographic area, which was the first mistake the Americans made—while they were numerically superior to the British, they were thinly stretched across the American defensive line. Vice Admiral Alexander Cochrane decided to use diversionary tactics to throw off the American defensive plans. The ruse worked successfully, and Major General Robert Ross successfully landed on Bladensburg with troops and artillery support. Colonel William Thornton led the British offensive to take the south bank of the Anacostia River. The American troops posted to guard the location fought back valiantly, but eventually, Thornton's forces took over the south bank, as well as the bridge that would get the British troops to the other side of the river to Lowndes Hill. The man who held the American defenses was Brigadier General Tobias Stansbury, and by the end of the battle, he had proven himself to be an incompetent commander.

After crossing the bridge to Lowndes Hill, Thornton's troops made a slow and steady approach, scattering the US troops in front of them with Congreve rockets, which they had successfully used before. At this point, the US troops were ordered to fall back, but confusion among the ranks resulted in many troops retreating and standing in formation again, allowing the British forces to overwhelm them easily. That doesn't mean the British had it easy; Commodore Joshua Barney, who was in charge of the American artillery, caused huge damage to the advancing British troops. Many historians argue that the Americans would have fared better if Fort Erie was still intact, but since it was lost, a retreat was the only option for the Americans. President Madison and his Cabinet also narrowly missed getting captured and fled from Washington, D.C., along with the other soldiers and civilians, to Brookeville.

That same night, the British forces entered the US capital, leading to the historic event known as the Burning of Washington. So far, this is the only instance of foreign troops invading the American capital since the American Revolution. Perhaps remembering the destruction the Americans caused at the Raid of Port Dover, the sappers and miners of the Corps of Royal Engineers started systematically burning down the principal government and civilian structures. The US Capitol was the first to be set ablaze, followed by the White House and other important establishments. The British soldiers captured all the supplies in the Washington Navy Yard and burned it as well. The way the fires were set would have taken days to put out, but luckily for the Americans, a terrible storm passed over the capital the very next day, putting out the fire and severely destroying many of the British ships.

From Washington, the British moved to the nearby town of Alexandria. The Raid on Alexandria, which lasted from August 29th to September 2nd, would have probably met the same fate as Washington if the mayor of the town didn't have the good sense to surrender, saving the town. Following the Burning of Washington, civilians and government officials slowly started returning to the charred capital. On September 19th, the US Congress assembled again at the Blodgett's Hotel, a building that housed the US Patent Office and one of the few surviving buildings that was large enough to hold all the members. After the War of 1812 was over, there was general outrage among American intellectuals that the burning of public buildings had been done out of pure spite and amounted to nothing more than vandalism. The British newspapers fired back, citing the same kind of damage done to York, Port Dover, and other Canadian settlements by American soldiers when they were victorious.

Chapter Five: The War of 1812- The Taming of the West

The invasion of Canada was only one part of the War of 1812. The Americans were fighting tooth and nail with the Native Americans in the newly acquired territories of Indiana and Illinois as well. Unlike the bitter defeats in the Canadian invasion, the Americans won many victories in the west from the very start, thanks to the brutal but effective command of William Henry Harrison, a man who would go on to become the future president of the United States. Unlike his northern counterparts, Harrison didn't mess around when building his forces. When the War of 1812 started, Harrison was already in charge of the Kentucky militia, who had a reputation of having the best sharpshooters in the country. Harrison didn't join the war during its first year as he was still serving as the governor of Kentucky. While he didn't fight, that didn't mean he was just sitting idly by— Fort Meigs, which would become an important strategic position in the War of 1812, was built along the Ohio River under his supervision. Harrison also had a fearful reputation among the Native Americans due to his massive success at the Battle of Tippecanoe in 1811. Not only had he disbanded the military might of Tecumseh's Native American alliance, but he had also broken their unity.

After Isaac Brock's death, Colonel Henry Procter stepped into his shoes, becoming Harrison's adversary. In terms of leadership and experience, Henry Procter was Isaac Brock's antithesis in many ways, a fact that has been compounded by Tecumseh's derision for Procter. While Brock was a decorated veteran with years of military and administrative experience under his belt, Procter had experience in neither field. The characters of both men were also starkly different—Brock was aggressive and a quick decision-maker while Procter was careful and slow to make decisions. Despite these differences, Procter ended up being a worthy successor to Brock in his own way.

About a month after the surrender of Fort Detroit on August 16th, 1812, the Siege of Fort Wayne took place, in which Harrison was partially involved. Lasting from September 5th to September 12th, the siege saw 500 Potawatomi and Miami warriors held back by 100 American soldiers until they were rescued by troops led by Harrison himself. Harrison moved with incredible speed to relieve Fort Wayne while increasing his forces along the way. By the time he reached the besieged fort, his army was 3,000 strong, more than capable enough to handle the Native American threat. Fortunately, the fort didn't suffer much damage as the Native Americans didn't possess artillery to breach the fort walls or gates.

The months of October and November 1812 largely consisted of naval conflicts in this region until November 22nd, which was when the Battle of Wild Cat Creek took place, which is located in Indiana. In response to the Pigeon Roost and Fort Dearborn massacres, the US government decided to take military action to suppress the Native Americans in the Illinois territory. Major General Samuel Hopkins and Colonel William Russell were put in charge of this expedition. But poor coordination and lack of accountability left the total campaign in shambles. At first, Colonel Russell pressed forward and managed to destroy a Kickapoo village near Peoria Lake. But when he failed to join up with Major General Hopkins, he was forced to retreat to Cahokia. Due to Russell's retreat, Hopkins had to retreat to Vincennes, which greatly angered him. After returning home from this failed attempt, Hopkins revamped his forces top to bottom, which included a company of regular infantry to make up for the lack of experience of the other troops as well as scouts. Setting out with this new army, Hopkins set out once again and marched as far as the site of the Battle of Tippecanoe. What Hopkins saw there enraged him and his troops. Many of the graves of the US soldiers who died in that battle were dug out and scalped, leaving a grotesque trail of bodies behind. After the bodies were buried again with proper rites, Hopkins and his men proceeded to the nearby Prophetstown, which had been partially rebuilt, and burned it down.

After this, Hopkins received reports from his scouts of a Winnebago village at the nearby Wild Cat Creek. US scouts had been ambushed upon being discovered by the local Native American warriors, who fled the scene and left behind the body of a soldier named Dunn. The following morning, on November 22nd, forces were sent to recover Dunn's body. Upon finding Dunn's head on a spike, thirteen of the enraged soldiers gave chase to a Native American warrior who acted as bait to lead the men into another ambush. The ambush caused twelve casualties in less than two minutes, prompting the rest of the American soldiers to flee quickly, with some dying in the retreat. After this ambush, Hopkins readied himself for a full-scale conflict, but his plans were deterred by the harsh winter. Some claim this battle holds little importance, but it helps to show that the US Army wanted to drive the Native Americans out of the area, something that could almost be considered an ulterior motive in the War of 1812.

In the late fall of 1812, William Henry Harrison started his campaign in the west. His plan was quite simple—to eradicate all Native American presence in the west as quickly as possible and then march on to liberate Detroit. Harrison used what is today known as scorched-earth tactics, which is where everything is razed behind the moving forces so that the land itself becomes unlivable. By doing this, an invading army can prevent enemy civilians or combatants from returning to that area. To make things easier for his fledgling army, Harrison ordered a military expedition against the Miami tribe in Indiana during his last days of governorship, which resulted in the Battle of the Mississinewa. Led by Lieutenant Colonel John Campbell, the 600 US cavalrymen were to attack Miami villages along the Mississinewa River and avoid harming the Miami chiefs. The first part of the expedition went smoothly, as the American forces captured three villages, starting with Lenape Chief Silver Heel's village, taking over 100 Lenape and Miami captives on December 17th. After being unable to proceed further due to the bad weather, Campbell deemed the campaign a success, and the American troops made their way back. However, when they reached Silver Heel's village once again the following morning, the American forces were ambushed by Native American warriors, who numbered to around 300. Campbell's forces were prepared, while the Native American counterattack was hastily put together. This resulted in an easy victory for the Americans, who killed 30 Native Americans and took 42 more as prisoners. After this battle, Campbell and his forces quickly made their way back to Fort Greenville with the prisoners. Even though Harrison touted this as a victory, when considered strategically, it was a loss. In the end, Campbell failed Harrison's intended goal, which was to cut off the Native American supplies to starve them during the winter.

As 1813 rolled in, the Americans saw more and more defeats until their first victory at Lake Erie in September (as this was a naval battle, it will be covered in the following chapter). It wasn't like the US wasn't winning any fights; they were, but the impact of those victories was very minimal. The main problem with the American war initiatives in 1813 was the same as that of the previous year—incompetent leadership. A random victory here and there didn't mean much when the commanders of the army were incompetent. Other than William Henry Harrison and Andrew Jackson, one would be hard-pressed to find solid commanders in this theater of the war. After a brief respite for a month, one of the most significant battles of the War of 1812 took place on January 18th, 1813. The Battle of Frenchtown, also known as the Battle of the River Raisin, took place in Frenchtown, Michigan Territory. A devastating blow to the US Army, this battle is often known as the River Raisin Massacre in history books.

Regaining Fort Detroit, which they had lost the year before, was vital for the American army in the War of 1812. As part of the strategy to recover Fort Detroit, the Americans attacked Frenchtown, a small settlement located 35 miles from Fort Detroit. The British-Canadian forces had captured this location the previous year, and Harrison now made this his stepping stone on his way to recovering Fort Detroit. The Battle of Frenchtown was by all accounts a large-scale war. There were two parts to the battle, and the numbers of the forces in the second part of the battle were fairly large: The American army numbered to around 1,000, while the British-Canadian-Native American forces consisted of 800 of Tecumseh's warriors and around 600 British regulars (it should be noted that while Tecumseh was in the area, he did not take part in this battle).

As stated, there were two skirmishes that took place over a period of five days, starting on January 18th. US Brigadier General James Winchester was ordered by William Henry Harrison to keep a safe distance from the main column led by Harrison and follow behind with a column of 1,000 troops that would act as a backup for the frontline troops. Instead of following Harrison's orders, Winchester decided to invade Frenchtown on his own, throwing Harrison's plans into shambles, even though it was a success. Led by Lieutenant Colonel William Lewis, about 700 men under Winchester's command surprised the small British regiment and the 200 Potawatomi that were garrisoned in the settlement. The fight was long and drawn-out, with a lot of close-quarters combat. But once the battle had ended, the British and Native American forces were in full retreat, leaving Frenchtown in Lewis' hands.

Though the American forces won the first round in the Battle of Frenchtown, modern historians and military tacticians agree that the victory was a fluke. Winchester's men were inexperienced, didn't follow a strategic plan, and were low in numbers. Though Harrison was pleased with Winchester's victory, he feared that the town might be reclaimed by the British due to the comparatively smaller number of soldiers in Winchester's detachment. His fears ultimately turned out to be true four days later. Hearing the news of the loss of the settlement, Brigadier General Henry Procter immediately set out for Michigan to reclaim it, leading a large force that was well-armed and well-supplied. The American army, on the other hand, had failed to reorganize themselves during the four-day interim between the two skirmishes. As a result, when Procter and his men struck at the Americans on January 22nd, they were caught completely off guard. Despite holding Frenchtown for several days, Lewis had ignored to post sentries around the clock. When the British and Native American forces attacked at dawn, the Americans were literally in their nightwear. The light American resistance lasted no longer than twenty minutes, giving Procter a decisive victory over the Americans. But the truly appalling part of the battle happened afterward when the Americans had already surrendered. The Americans had suffered huge losses—around 400 lay dead, more than 40 men were wounded, and 547 men were taken as prisoners. In effect, Winchester's whole force was wiped out.

Harrison's actions to subdue the Native American population had garnered him and his men much animosity from the Native American tribes in general, not just the Miami. So, when the Native Americans warriors finally got their hands on Harrison's soldiers, it was a total massacre. On the one hand, they had shown admirable restraint when they refused to burn down Frenchtown according to Procter's suggestion, as they wanted to avoid civilian bloodshed. But Harrison's soldiers were a totally different story. Procter wanted to avoid American retaliation that he knew was soon to come, so he decided to retreat back to Fort Malden the very next day, leaving the American prisoners who were too wounded to make the trek with him at the mercy of the Native Americans. On January 23rd, one of the most brutal Native American massacres took place in the River Raisin. First, fire was set on the wooden houses containing the wounded American prisoners. The smell of flesh and burning wood mingled with the anguished screams of wounded American soldiers, which filled the air in moments. The soldiers who managed to get out of the buildings were hacked brutally with machetes and scalped. The few British soldiers who were left behind did absolutely nothing out of sheer terror. Only when Tecumseh arrived on the scene and stopped his brethren did the brutality stop. Estimates of those killed range between 30 and 100.

Two weeks after the Battle of Frenchtown, the US Army saw some minor success by raiding Elizabethtown, which was located in Upper Canada. Major Benjamin Forsyth led a small company of 200 men and successfully raided the settlement twice before retreating back to American soil. His actions, however, caught the eye of George Prévost, who immediately laid out plans to take over Ogdensburg, which Forsyth was using as his forward base. The British had already tried to take Ogdensburg, which was about 22 miles from Elizabethtown, in October of 1812, but it had failed; now, they were going to try again. On February 22nd, 1813, Lieutenant Colonel George MacDonell led a desperate charge across the frozen St. Lawrence River toward Ogdensburg. The American army was taken completely by surprise but immediately fired upon the advancing British troops. Though they did manage to do some damage, the British forces ultimately swarmed the American artillery, forcing the American troops to retreat to the civilian quarters. After a drawn-out battle, in which Forsyth's artillery commanders were both wounded, the American troops finally surrendered. Though the Battle of Ogdensburg was a small skirmish, it was an important victory for the British forces, as they had successfully managed to eliminate an important threat to their supply lines. The following few months mostly consisted of naval conflicts while the land troops on both sides recuperated.

After the stunning defeat at the Battle of York in April 1813, the Canadian military decided to attack Fort Meigs, the fortification William Henry Harrison had built during his last days as governor. Within a few short months, Fort Meigs had proven itself to be an important strategic location along the Maumee River, necessitating its attack. Tecumseh and Major General Henry Procter, the respective leaders of the Native American and British forces, were both present during this attack, signifying its importance. But at the same time, this was also the battle that caused a significant rift between the British and Native American military alliance. The Native Americans had made up the bulk of the British ground troops in the previous battles of the War of 1812, and this would be the last time they would do so.

This siege began on April 28th, and it took several days for the British forces to move into position. Tecumseh and Wyandot Chief Roundhead spearheaded the assault with 1,250 Native American troops, while the British-Canadian troops led by Procter numbered to around 900. Harrison, on the other hand, had 2,800 men at his command, who were all safe inside the fort. Taking advantage of this, Harrison decided to wear out his opponents by simply making no moves at all. On the morning of May 5th, the Americans sent Colonel William Dudley and Colonel John Miller to sabotage the British cannons on the north and south end of the British positions. Dudley and his 866 men successfully reached their target in the north and were in the middle of disabling the British cannon when some of his men were baited by Tecumseh's warriors into the woods. In a desperate attempt to stop them, Dudley gave chase, leaving a small detachment under his second-in-command, Major James Shelby. While Dudley was giving chase in the woods, Shelby's force was wiped out from a counterattack by British Major Adam Muir, who attacked with three regiments of troops. Dudley was killed in the first few minutes of battle. Most of his men were either taken as prisoner or killed. Only 150 men from Dudley's failed assault managed to make it back to Fort Meigs. Miller was successful in his attempt, capturing the battery and prisoners, but he suffered heavy losses on his way back to the fort.

Despite this overwhelming British victory, Procter refused to capitalize on it and mount an offensive on the fort to Tecumseh's great frustration. Seeing how things were, a formal prisoner exchange was conducted between the American and the British, and the British abandoned the siege on May 9th, 1813. Many military historians argue that if Procter had more military experience and was more decisive like Isaac Brock, this might have been a major British victory instead of an American one. Though the Americans had taken more casualties in this battle, they had managed to retain their position, which was a big win in the War of 1812.

Chapter Six: The War of 1812- The Creek War

While the War of 1812 started separately with the invasion of Canada as well as the western theater of the war, in a strange twist of fate, the Creek War in the south also became a part of the overall conflict. It started alongside Tecumseh's War in 1810, but it wasn't until 1813 when the Red Stick Creeks declared war on the US Army. The man who held the helm of the American forces in the Creek War was Andrew Jackson, a novice commander who would prove his mettle in his very first campaign and would turn him into a veteran Native American fighter by the end of it. Jackson's victories were crucial in maintaining the balance in the War of 1812 due to the disastrous performance of the US military in most of the land conflicts. The Red Stick Creeks were a rising threat, and had they been left unchecked in the War of 1812, the combined pressure of the Red Sticks and the British might have been enough for the Americans to surrender. Fortunately for the US, that did not happen, and the American commanders in the north and the west were able to keep up the fight until the end of the war. The Spanish in Florida helped the Red Sticks a great deal by providing them with weapons and ammunition, a fact that would greatly anger Andrew Jackson.

While many of the Native American tribes in North America were distrustful of Western culture and religion, the Creek in the south were very welcoming of the new culture. Many of them turned into Christians, adopted American clothing, and developed a taste for American vices, such as drinking and gambling. All of this created a tense atmosphere within the Creek tribes themselves, which caused a social rift. (It should be noted that the Creek were not one single tribe; they were a group of related tribes in the southeast.) Many of the elders of the Creek tribes became disdainful of how Western culture invaded theirs, and they started demanding reformations within the confederacy. The problems became more pronounced as the Americans started encroaching more and more on Creek land in the south, ignoring the protests of the tribes living on the land. When Tecumseh came to them in the early 19th century to take them under the wing of his brother's religious movement, the response was split. Many of the Creek, specifically the Lower Creek tribes, responded to Tecumseh's invitation eagerly. The more progressive tribes saw him as something of a troublemaker and refused to ally themselves with him. But Tecumseh gained further support in 1811 when he delivered an anti-Anglo speech at the Creek council at Tukabatchee, which drew a crowd of 50,000 Creeks. His speech was very well received among the Creek tribes, drawing them more into a militant position against the US Army and government. The Creek who decided to answer Tecumseh's call for war started to become known as the Red Stick Creeks around this point.

The Creek War is outlined by three American campaigns—the Mississippi campaign, the North Carolina and South Carolina campaign, and the Tennessee campaign. The first two campaigns were failures, even though they weren't outright defeats. The American army did gain the upper hand in the Tennessee campaign, which was led by Andrew Jackson. Jackson's campaign was a direct response to the Fort Mims massacre, which saw the largest number of civilian deaths in the War of 1812 and shook the American government and public to their core. After the Americans burned Spanish supplies that were given to the Red Sticks, the Red Sticks retaliated back with the massacre at Fort Mims. Fort Mims was occupied by 265 militia, which was a considerable number for defensive purposes, but the Red Sticks under William Weatherford (also known as Red Eagle) and Peter McQueen had between 750 to 1,000 warriors in their ranks. The Red Sticks attacked at midday and charged straight through the main gate. The speed of the attack overwhelmed the American soldiers guarding the main gate. Once they gained access to the fort, the Red Sticks started massacring civilians and soldiers alike. All 265 militia were either killed or captured, and 252 civilians (out of 517) were killed or captured.

To control the situation, Tennessee Governor Willie Blount ordered Andrew Jackson to prepare for a campaign to subdue the Red Sticks, as well as take actions against the Spanish who had already become a thorn in America's side. The Tennessee campaign didn't exactly set off on a positive note. When Jackson decided to mobilize his troops on October 10th, 1813, for the Tennessee expedition, he was initially slowed down for many reasons. The Tennessee River had a low tide, making it difficult for Jackson to gather and move his supplies in tandem with his troops. On top of that, the recruitment for his expedition was not complete yet, forcing Jackson to set out under Governor Blount's orders with only 2,500 troops. The first thing Jackson did after setting out was establish Fort Strother as his supply base, a decision that would prove to be useful. Almost three weeks after setting out, Jackson faced his first major challenge in the Battle of Tallushatchee. While Jackson was establishing Fort Strother along the Coosa River, his scouts reported a Red Sticks encampment fifteen miles north. In what can be simply described as overkill, General John Coffee, one of Jackson's close friends and officers, took around 900 cavalrymen to burn the Red Sticks encampment to the ground, killing 186 of them in the process.

Richard K. Call, one of the participants in the Battle of Tallushatchee, later described the event in his memoirs:

> The next morning after our march we entered the Indian village, and here I first saw the carnage of the battle field. I saw it in its worst aspect—when the hour of danger had passed, when I could excite no feeling or passion in my breast, to control my sympathy and sorrow for human suffering. It was to me a horrible and revolting scene—the battle had ended in the village, the warriors fighting in their board houses, which gave little protection against the rifle bullets or musket ball. They fought in the midst of their wives and children, who frequently shared their bloody fate. They fought bravely to the last, none asking or receiving quarter, nor did resistance cease until the last warrior had fallen. Humanity might well have wept over the gory scene before us. We found as many as eight or ten dead bodies in a single cabin, sometimes the dead mother clasped the dead child to her breast, and to add another appalling horror to the bloody catalogue—some of the cabins had taken fire, and half consumed human bodies were seen amidst the smoking ruins. In other instances dogs had torn and feasted on the mangled bodies of their masters. Heartsick I turned from the revolting scene. Very different seems the picture in the cool moment of inaction than in the excitement of battle—in the one—passion, the desire to triumph, and vengeance make demons, in the other as the brain becomes more composed, the pulse to beat less quickly, the heart resumes its sway—and it would be a relief to shed tears over the carnage around us—I remember an instance of a brave young soldier, who after fighting like a tiger until the engagement was over, fainted at the sight of the blood he has helped to spill.

On November 9th, six days after the Battle of Tallushatchee, Andrew Jackson won his second military victory in the Battle of Talladega. Soon after Coffee's victory in the Battle of Tallushatchee, some of the Upper Creek asked for Jackson's help to stop the Red Sticks at Talladega. The Red Sticks had become violent to the point where they were burning and killing their own people if they didn't agree with the Red Sticks' militant views and policies. This time around, Jackson himself led his forces, which consisted of 2,000 infantry and cavalrymen. The Red Sticks led by Red Eagle, also known as William Weatherford, were 700 strong. Like the Battle of Tallushatchee, the Battle of Talladega was also a comparatively short and straightforward affair devoid of any advanced tactics. As soon as Jackson and his forces appeared in front of the village of Talladega, they were attacked by the Red Sticks. Jackson's forces retaliated back and overwhelmed the Red Sticks within a very short amount of time. Jackson's forces only suffered 15 deaths while the Red Sticks had 300, making this a decisive first victory for Jackson. But Jackson had a very difficult time managing his forces throughout the month of December. Around 500 men deserted his forces, which was a severe blow to Jackson, as he had just lost one-fifth of his army. Supplies were low, as was the men's morale. Despite facing these difficult situations, Jackson marched to aid the Georgia militia in January, which cumulated in the Battles of Emuckfaw and Enotachopo Creek.

The conditions for the Battles of Emuckfaw and Enotachopo Creek were unfavorable for Jackson. The enlistment period of the troops who had fought the first few skirmishes with Jackson in 1813 were going to expire by mid-January. As a result, when Jackson marched for the Battles of Emuckfaw and Enotachopo Creek, he was marching with 900 fresh militia recruits who had no experience or training to fight the Red Sticks menace. The first battle took place near Emuckfaw on January 22nd, 1814. Jackson and his forces were camped a few miles away from Emuckfaw when the Red Sticks suddenly attacked at dawn. After half an hour of fighting, the Red Sticks were beaten back, at which point Jackson sent Coffee with 400 men to lead a counterattack on the Red Stick camp. After seeing the Red Stick numbers, Coffee decided to fall back, which gave the

Red Sticks another opportunity to attack Jackson's camp. This time around, Coffee was badly wounded, forcing Jackson to make the tough decision to retreat. Jackson was a realist and understood that without experienced men on his side, fighting the Red Sticks on an equal footing was not a possibility. So, he collected his forces and headed for Fort Strother. However, the Red Sticks weren't done with Jackson and attacked his forces again on January 24th as they were crossing Enotachopo Creek. Jackson's forces managed to mount a counterattack, which wasn't very effective as the rearguard panicked and retreated. For some unknown reason, the Red Sticks decided not to push forward with their attack, allowing Jackson and his men to retreat safely. As such, these battles had no clear winner; while Jackson was forced to retreat, the Red Sticks did not gain any major victory out the battles. After these battles, Jackson waited out in Fort Strother until Governor Blount made good on his promise and sent 2,500 troops to Jackson to continue the Tennessee campaign.

Another case of an American retreat from the Red Sticks took place during the Battle of Calebee Creek, located in present-day Macon County, Alabama. This skirmish took place on the night of January 27th, 1814, when 1,300 Red Sticks led by Red Eagle ambushed John Floyd's forces of 1,200 volunteer militia and 400 Yuchi allies. Floyd was deployed alongside Jackson with the same objective—to defeat the Red Sticks. The Red Sticks had been tracking Floyd's movement for some time before the skirmish took place. Red Eagle and his forces attacked Floyd's forces at dawn, throwing the entire company into disarray. But the American forces fought back fiercely, causing heavy casualties on both sides. After an hour of fighting, Floyd's forces managed to beat the Red Sticks back. But despite the victory, many modern historians tend to agree that Floyd's forces suffered the worst of the attack.

On March 27th, 1814, the final battle of the Creek War took place, the Battle of Horseshoe Bend. This battle skyrocketed Andrew Jackson into fame. After the Battle of Calebee Creek, the Red Sticks decided to make their final stand and started gathering troops by the

Tallapoosa River. After receiving his reinforcement of 2,500 men in February, Jackson once again started preparations to attack the Red Sticks. Fortunately for him, their Native American allies, the Cherokee and Creek, also joined his forces in this battle, giving Jackson a much-needed boost in numbers, as most of his men were inexperienced in fighting. To better organize his plans, Jackson decided to move to Fort Williams prior to the attack. The Red Stick army was led by their chief Menawa, and they were camped at Horseshoe Bend near the banks of the Tallapoosa River. Numbering at around 1,000 warriors, the Red Sticks hadn't finished assimilating their full force, which gave Jackson a huge tactical advantage in this battle.

Putting his trust in his best friend again, Jackson ordered Brigadier General John Coffee to cross the river and surround the camp from the south side with 700 men, while Jackson would cover the north side of the camp. After all his men had been positioned, Jackson ordered his artillery units to start bombarding the village at 10:30 in the morning. But the Red Sticks had built good defenses that weren't affected by the artillery fire. Seeing that the results were not satisfactory, Jackson ordered a bayonet charge into the village. Led by Colonel John Williams of the 39th US Infantry, the bayonet charge was a success, and the American troops were finally able to cross the Red Stick defenses and enter the village. This started a brutal close-quarters combat situation that went on for some time (about five hours). Once the defenses were penetrated, Coffee also led his charge at the same time, overwhelming the Red Sticks from both the front and back. The Red Sticks offered no surrender, and every last man in the camp was either killed or wounded, effectively putting an end to the Creek War.

After this battle, the Native American tribes in the area were forced to sign the Treaty of Fort Jackson, which saw the US government acquire 23 million acres of land. Since Jackson was the man responsible for acquiring this treaty, he was promoted to the rank of major general soon afterward. As the Red Sticks had been completely subdued, Jackson now turned his eyes on Pensacola, which eventually culminated in the Battle of New Orleans. The preparations took some time as Jackson had sent Captain John Gordon to verify whether the British were actually coordinating with the Spanish or not. After weeks of hard traveling, Gordon came back and reported that Jackson's suspicions were true. Upon discovering this, Jackson started to prepare for his campaign against the Spanish.

The Battle of Pensacola was a relatively short and straightforward affair compared to Jackson's previous victories. Jackson's plan was to conquer Spanish Florida and move on to New Orleans to defend the city from further attacks. After being joined by Brigadier General John Coffee and raising 4,000 troops, Jackson finally set out for his expedition to Pensacola on November 2nd. Upon arriving, Jackson didn't immediately engage and instead sent Major Henri Piere to the city to negotiate a surrender. But to Jackson's chagrin, Major Piere was shot and killed when he was passing Fort San Miguel. Jackson sent a second envoy, who survived the trip but came back with the news that Spanish Governor Mateo González Manrique refused to surrender. So, Jackson started his assault on Pensacola on November 7th. He attacked at dawn, and to reduce casualties, he ordered 1,000 of his troops to flank Pensacola from the beach where the Spanish cannon fire couldn't reach. With the other 3,000 troops, Jackson marched into the city himself. He managed to reach the center of the city and capture the artillery batteries that were peppering his troops with fire. Manrique offered to surrender following this drastic turn of events. The following day, Fort San Miguel surrendered to the American troops. Jackson was still unappeased and decided to launch a final assault the following day, but before he could act, a huge explosion destroyed the city of Pensacola. This prompted the British to retreat, along with some of their Spanish allies, giving Jackson an easy victory, albeit an empty one. Despite two days of fighting, the casualties on both sides were fairly minimal—the Americans only suffered seven killed and eleven wounded while the British and Spanish suffered fifteen casualties.

The Battle of New Orleans is arguably the last major military action in the War of 1812. Technically, this battle shouldn't have happened since the Treaty of Ghent had already been signed by both the American and the British. But back in those days, it took time for news to reach one end of the country to the other. After his victory in Pensacola, Jackson quickly moved to New Orleans as fast as possible after hearing news of British troops advancing toward the city. The British forces, led by Major General Sir Edward Pakenham, attacked New Orleans on January 8th, 1815. Despite the huge number of troops led by Pakenham (8,000), the Americans under Jackson won an easy victory. In a way, the Battle of New Orleans was the exact opposite of the Battle of Bladensburg—every mistake the Americans made in that battle was more or less repeated by the British in this battle. Jackson had 5,700 men under his command and used them strategically to beat back the British Army. The British Army attacked at dawn to take advantage of the fog and poor line of sight, but this ended up being a fatal mistake as the fog cleared when the British infantry columns reached the range of enemy musket fire. The attacking forces led two assaults against the American defensive line and were beaten back both times. During the second attack, both Pakenham and his second-in-command, Major General Samuel Gibbs, were injured after being hit by a grapeshot round, which led to their deaths later on. The loss of their commanders, as well as the heavy losses they were taking, prompted the British to retreat. They would later try to make a naval assault on the city but were deterred from that plan as well. After this battle, the War of 1812 officially ended, and the few small naval skirmishes here and there were largely ignored by both sides.

Chapter Seven: The War of 1812- Naval Battles of the War of 1812

So far, we have discussed the land battles of the War of 1812; now, we will discuss the naval battles, which upset the tide of the war on more than one occasion, the most famous one being the Battle of Lake Erie. The naval battles of this war were between two altogether different maritime forces. Britain had perhaps the world's best naval force at the time, while the United States came up short with their fighting armada. The difference in quality of the two sides can be explained. The United States was still a fairly new country at the time, and there were many other important issues, such as establishing a strong government, that took precedence. As such, the United States did not have the time to create a strong navy, let alone one that could compare with Great Britain. Instead, the United States mainly used their navy for trade. Great Britain, on the other hand, had utilized their naval forces over the centuries for warfare. Since Great Britain is located on an island, it was of tremendous importance that their navy be strong.

When the War of 1812 started, it was automatically assumed by the Americans that most of the war would be fought on land, which prompted barely any enthusiasm for recruitment in the US Navy. After all, the American navy was a fledgling force, and no logical commander would think that the Americans had a fighting chance against the British on water. Ironically, it was in the naval battles that the Americans claimed some of their biggest victories in the War of 1812. When discussing the naval battles, it's important to remember the battles were fought in the Atlantic Ocean and various lakes. In fact, it was the inland naval battles that brought the more prolific American victories than the ones at sea, which were mostly limited to capturing enemy ships.

Considering the poor condition of the US Navy, it is logical to question as to how they managed to win so many naval conflicts. The answer to that question is simple—privateers. The act of using pirates and other criminals as a subsidized naval force is nothing new in the history of naval warfare, and such was the case in the War of 1812. The privateers in the War of 1812 were basically merchant ships outfitted with small guns. As a result, they were able to maintain better maneuverability than the British. Yet despite their numerous successes, the privateers ultimately failed to crack the multiple naval blockades that the British enforced in the second and third years of the war. The British also engaged privateers of their own for the blockades, who were active in the regions of Nova Scotia, New Brunswick, and Bermuda. These regions were comparatively safer for the British ships.

At the beginning of the War of 1812, the Royal Navy suffered some major problems. It might have been one of the largest fleets in Europe at the time, but that, in itself, would pose an issue. All those ships needed men to man them, men that Great Britain did not have. Not only were they fighting a war in America, but the Napoleonic Wars were still in full swing over in Europe. As such, Great Britain had to hastily recruit, as well as impress, men. This led to poorly trained seamen who had trouble holding their own against the more experienced men onboard the American ships. The British ships themselves were less powerful than their American counterparts as well. For instance, one of the most famous naval battles in the War of 1812 was between the USS *Constitution* and the HMS *Guerriere*. The USS *Constitution* had 56 guns and a crew of 480. The HMS *Guerriere*, on the other hand, had 44 guns and only 272 men manning it. Although the battle between the two ships was intense, in the end, the USS *Constitution*'s double-shotted guns were able to demast the HMS *Guerriere*.

In addition to Britain's other problems was the lack of materials and skilled shipwrights. Without the required materials and skilled hands needed to fix the ships, the British ships had begun to slowly deteriorate and underperform over the years. The Americans, however, could rely on local dockyards that were fully equipped and supplied. These dockyards produced tougher ships and heavier guns compared to the British fleet, a prime example being the USS *United States'* capture of the HMS *Macedonian*. The USS *United States* had the new American "heavy frigate" design, while the HMS *Macedonian* was of the older British Lively-class frigate design. While the British ship had a larger assortment of armaments, the speed advantage of the American ship was overwhelming for a ship of that size. The American guns had, most of the time, double the destructive power of the regular British cannons, which allowed them to cause significantly more damage while carrying fewer guns. Essentially, the American naval strategy was hit first and hit hard. This proved to be extremely effective, as demonstrated by the early American naval victories in 1812.

When the USS *Constitution* took down the HMS *Guerriere* on August 19th, 1812, both sides were surprised by the sudden American victory. Before the battle began, the *Constitution* had caught sight of an unknown ship, and US Captain Isaac Hull decided to check it out. Prior to this skirmish, the *Constitution* had faced a large British fleet but managed to escape; coincidentally, the HMS *Guerriere* had also been in that fleet. When the ships got close enough, they recognized each other's flags and immediately prepared for combat.

At first, the *Guerriere* gave chase to the *Constitution*, firing its broadside cannons to little effect, as the strong wind ruined the shots. The chase went on for 45 minutes until a cannonball bounced off the side of the *Constitution* without causing any damage; after this battle, the ship went on to be known as "Old Ironsides." Emboldened by the lack of damage to their ship, the sailors on the *Constitution* closed the distance between the two ships in order to take advantage of its heavier guns more effectively. The *Guerriere* stayed still, confident that its size and heavy weaponry would destroy the incoming ship. When both of the ships came within point-blank range of each other, they began exchanging fire in earnest.

The fight dragged on for fifteen minutes or so with little damage to the *Constitution*. But the British ship was not aware that the *Constitution* possessed heavy guns and a strong hull, which ended up being their undoing. The mizzenmast of the *Guerriere* was destroyed by a cannon shot from the *Constitution*, which caused the *Guerriere* to lose balance. The *Constitution* took advantage of the *Guerriere*'s distress and positioned itself at the exposed front of the *Guerriere*. The men on the *Constitution* delivered a punishing barrage of cannon fire, raking the *Guerriere* so badly that the ship lost its mainmast, leaving it totally immobile. The *Constitution* came around for a second charge, but the ships became tangled in the process, necessitating hand-to-hand combat. Although boarding parties were formed on both the *Guerriere* and the *Constitution*, neither side was able cross to the other due to the extensive damage caused.

Once both captains realized that boarding the other ship was not an option, they both started firing their cannons again, despite being precariously tangled. The *Guerriere* tried to escape the fight, but given the heavily damaged condition of the ship, this proved to be impossible. The *Constitution*, however, managed to untangle itself briefly and was able to make some repairs before starting to attack the *Guerriere* once more. British Captain James Dacres, who was wounded in the fight, realized his ship would not survive another attack like that and signaled his surrender by having a cannon fired in the opposite direction of the *Constitution*. When Captain Hull sent a small boat to confirm whether the enemy was surrendering or not, Dacres famously responded to the men on the boat, "Well, Sir, I don't know. Our mizzenmast is gone, our fore and main masts are gone—I think on the whole you might say we have struck our flag."

On the American side, the casualties amounted to seven killed and seven wounded. The British suffered significantly more damage, with 15 killed, 78 wounded, and the remaining 257 captured. Although Hull wanted to take the *Guerriere* as a prize ship, it had been immobilized, so the Americans set fire to it before they left for Boston with the news, which helped to positively impact morale.

The American naval successes in 1812, such as the USS *Essex* versus HMS *Alert*, USS *Wasp* (1807) versus HMS *Frolic*, and USS *Wasp* (1807) versus HMS *Poictiers* (1809), among others, caused a huge uproar in Britain; they simply couldn't figure out why the superior British ships were being taken down one after another by these upstart Yankees, who had smaller ships and barely any firepower. On February 18th, 1813, George Canning, who once was the treasurer of the navy as well as the foreign secretary, told the House of Commons that "the sacred spell of the invincibility of the British Navy was broken."

The British had a right to be concerned, as they still had one of the biggest naval battles to contend with, the Battle of Lake Erie. When the War of 1812 first broke out, Oliver Hazard Perry was sent out to take control of the American fleet on Lake Erie. When he landed on Presque Isle, Michigan, a few craftsmen were already charged to create a small fleet for him that would be suitable for the inland water bodies. After one year, he had nine ships at the ready. Seven of his new fleet vessels were gunboats, small vessels with the mounting capacity of just one cannon. Just two, the *Lawrence* and the *Niagara*, were full-sized ships that accommodated two long guns and eighteen carronades, a short-caliber cannon. Perry had also gathered a dedicated group of 500 men, and following months of hard training, they were a proficient maritime unit ready for war with the British.

In September 1813, Perry sailed to Put-In-Bay, Ohio, to face off against the British armada, which was commanded by Robert Heriot Barclay. The British had started developing an armada at Lake Erie almost at the same time as Perry. Before the battle, both sides were scurrying like ants to build their fleet quickly. In the end, it was the British fleet that launched first into the lake. On September 10th, 1813, the Battle of Lake Erie occurred. It seemed as if the Americans held the advantage from the beginning since they had nine ships compared to Britain's two. But from the get-go, the British ships hammered the American ones with their long guns, which were more accurate. At one point, the British successfully pulverized the *Lawrence*, the ship that Perry was on. Perry grabbed the ship's banner and moved to the *Niagara* with great danger to himself. After Perry had moved ships, the Americans started to win the fight. Prior to Perry's appearance on the *Niagara*, this ship had barely drawn any of the British fire since their focus was on Perry's ship. Taking advantage of this situation, the *Niagara*, now under Perry's direct command, caused overwhelming damage to the British-occupied *Lawrence* (the British took it over once Perry abandoned it) with its heavy guns. The commanders of almost all of the British ships were slaughtered or injured, leaving the British ships under the command of inexperienced officers who were scared and confused. Perry exploited this circumstance, slamming the *Niagara* into Barclay's damaged ships. It managed to break through the line of British ships and came into firing range of the HMS *Detroit* and *Queen Charlotte*. The sailors aboard the smaller American vessels focused on firing upon these British ships as well. These two ships surrendered around 3 p.m., and the smaller ships, which tried to flee, were overtaken. Forty-one British were killed, 93 were wounded, and 306 were captured, which meant that none of the British who participated in this battle escaped unscathed.

Perry sent a message to Major General William Henry Harrison, detailing the fight with great enthusiasm and exaggeration. In the letter, he wrote, "We have met the foe, and they are our own."

The American triumph at the Battle of Lake Erie was a big achievement, as the Americans now controlled Lake Erie. With the removal of the British stockpile lines, Fort Detroit was theirs once again. It additionally prepared for General Harrison's assault on the British and Native American powers at the Battle of the Thames, in which Tecumseh met his untimely demise.

One of the last big naval battles, the Battle of Plattsburgh, took place in 1814. This battle included both land and naval forces, with the naval forces overseen by US Master Commandant Thomas Macdonough and British Captain George Downie. George Prévost, who was in charge of the British land forces, arrived at Plattsburgh on September 6th, 1814, but didn't attack right away, instead focusing on strengthening his position. It was Prévost's hope that once Downie attacked the American ships in Plattsburgh Bay, the generals on land would coordinate to begin a full-on assault against the Americans.

Captain George Downie was unable to place the frigate *Confiance* in the place he desired; however, he still managed to launch a broadside that killed or wounded one-fifth of the crew on the USS *Saratoga*, Thomas Macdonough's flagship. Macdonough may have been stunned by the blast, but he didn't let it stop him for long. A few minutes later, the *Saratoga* fired, killing Downie in the process. Two of the British sloops, *Chubb* and *Finch*, surrendered soon after this, leaving the brig *Linnet*, as well as the *Confiance*, the main ships left in the fray. The USS *Saratoga* and the *Confiance* slowly brought each other to a standstill, with most of the officers on board the *Confiance* either dead or injured while the majority of the guns on the *Saratoga* were out of action. Macdonough ordered the *Saratoga*'s bow anchor to be cut, allowing the ship to spin around and bringing its undamaged guns into action. With the *Confiance* unable to return fire, it was forced to surrender. The *Linnet* followed soon after, as the *Saratoga* battered it heavily.

Although the land battle was supposed to start at the same time, it took a little bit longer to get underway. However, since the

Americans were victorious on the water, there was no reason for the British to go ahead with their assault, and they retreated as soon as they heard the news of the naval battle. The American and British were already meeting to discuss the Treaty of Ghent at this point, and this battle helped to cement the American position. If the British had been successful, they could have had more leverage in demanding to keep more of the territories they had gained during the war. Instead, the treaty essentially wiped the slate clean, restoring the borders of the two countries to what it had been before the war.

Conclusion

By the time the War of 1812 had reached its third year, both sides were starting to get eager to conclude the war as soon as possible. The cost of the war was mounting for the US, and the British were getting increasingly agitated after the long string of defeats in 1813. To make peace, both the US and Great Britain decided to send envoys to neutral ground to negotiate the terms of peace. Belgium was chosen as the neutral ground, and in August 1814, delegates from both sides arrived at Ghent to negotiate a treaty. In the beginning, both sides overwhelmed each other with impossible demands—the Americans demanded that Canada be integrated into America, while the British demanded a Native American buffer state. Understandably, both these demands were impossible to meet, and the delegates argued for weeks on these topics. Giving up Canada would mean zero control in North America for the British, and creating a Native American buffer state would impede American expansion in the west.

While the discussions were underway, the British had a couple of invasions planned out, so it is logical to assume that they had different goals in mind and were stalling the treaty to let those incursions play out. The American delegates, on the other hand, were also playing the same game—they were hoping that France would again raise a ruckus in Europe to distract the British. The negotiations played back and forth for four months, and to the surprise of both parties, their months of stalling ended up being useless. France didn't rise to arms again, and the British invasions had negative results. Seeing the situation for what it was, both parties decided on reestablishing the old North American borders before the war, including lands that were wrested from the Native Americans as well. On December 24th, 1814, both sides agreed upon the conditions of the treaty and went back to their respective countries. The Treaty of Ghent was ratified by both governments by February, formally ending the war. But it wasn't until a few months later that the war was actually over, as a small local battle known as the Battle of the Sink Hole took place between the American army and Sauk forces.

Looking at it from a modern perspective, the War of 1812 was perhaps the most pointless war in American history. The number of lives lost and the expenses made to fund the war effort drained American resources significantly. And to top it all off, they were left standing in the same position as they were three years ago, with no change in geographic lines. Also, the Treaty of Ghent nullified all the Native American land that the Americans had acquired as well. This resulted in a century-long conflict against the Native American population, which saw numerous casualties and brutalities on both sides. So, in a way, this war did more harm than good, as the aftermath was a political fiasco in regards to Native American relations since many of the Americans who participated in this war would go on to acquire important government and military positions. These men had accrued a deep hatred for the Native American population during the Creek War and the War of 1812, which ultimately drove them to subjugate the Native American population at all costs. And to make matters worse, they would go on to pass their ideologies on to the next generation, who would continue the cycle of brutality.

But there were some positive results of this war. After this war, the United States and Britain were closer than ever before. Although the two countries hit a few rough patches in the 1860s, their relationship is still strong to this day. Another positive outcome of the war was a trained standing US Army and Navy. The concept of a trained standing army was already in practice by 1814, but afterward, it became the norm. After analyzing their poor performance in most of the battles of the War of 1812, the American military came to the conclusion that the difference between them and the British forces was training. Many of the Canadian militia had been trained by British regulars during the war and, as a result, performed better than the average American militiaman. The American navy was also reorganized and superbly outfitted due to its amazing performance in the War of 1812. One could argue that if it wasn't for the US Navy, the War of 1812 would have ended much sooner and with an American defeat.

The War of 1812 also has profound significance in Canadian and Native American history. For the Canadians, this was the war that led them to discover their own identity. They weren't British or Americans; they were Canadians. Thus, many of the British heroes of the war ended up being Canadian heroes, the most prominent of them being Isaac Brock. For the Native Americans, this was the beginning of the fall of their power in North America. The Creek War had seen tensions rise between American settlers and Native Americans, which dramatically increased when the Native Americans sided with the British. Tecumseh's death was also a huge blow for the Native Americans, especially those tribes in the north— he was to be their savior, but his untimely death in the Battle of the Thames helped to start a dark chapter in Native American history. The British Empire was also radically changed by this war as well— after decades of fighting in Europe, which had taken a toll on Britain's resources, the British finally focused their attention on India to more fully expand their empire.

Here are other books by Captivating History that you might be interested in

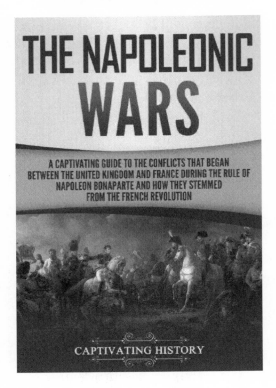

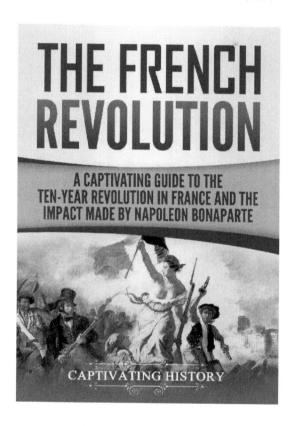

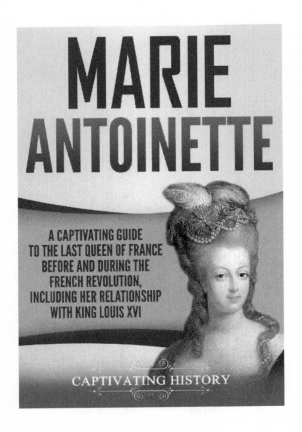

References:

"War of 1812-1815." Office of the Historian, Bureau of Public Affairs, United States Department of State, history.state.gov/milestones/1801-1829/war-of-1812

Bickham, Troy. The Weight of Vengeance: The United States, The British Empire and The War of 1812. Oxford University Press, 2012.

Springer, Paul J. "The Causes of the War of 1812." Foreign Policy Research Institute, 31 March. 2017, www.fpri.org/article/2017/03/causes-war-1812/

Borneman, Walter. 1812: The War That Forged a Nation. Harper Perennial, 2004.

Taylor, Alan. The Civil War of 1812: American Citizens, British Subjects, Irish Rebels, & Indian Allies. Vintage Books, 2010.

"Two Wars for Independence." American Battlefield Trust, www.battlefields.org/learn/articles/two-wars-independence

"The War of 1812 Could Have Been the War of Indian Independence." Indian Country Today, 17 May. 2017, newsmaven.io/indiancountrytoday/archive/the-war-of-1812-could-have-been-the-war-of-indian-independence-NgDgX3JKHEaPWtiUIyMxBA/

"Entanglement in World Affairs." The Mariner's Museum, www.marinersmuseum.org/sites/micro/usnavy/08/08d.htm

Brunsman, Denver. The Evil Necessity: British Naval Impressment in the Eighteenth Century Atlantic World. University of Virginia Press, 2013.

Deeben, John P. "The War of 1812: Stoking the Fires." National Archives, www.archives.gov/publications/prologue/2012/summer/1812-impressment.html

Sweeney, Alastair. Fire Along the Frontier: Great Battles of the War of 1812. Dundurn Press, 2012.

Foreman, Amanda. "The British View the War of 1812 Quite Differently Than Americans Do." Smithsonian Magazine, Smithsonian Institute, July. 2014, www.smithsonianmag.com/history/british-view-war-1812-quite-differently-americans-do-180951852/

Campbell, Duncan Andrew (2015). "The Bicentennial of the War of 1812: Reconsidering the "Forgotten Conflict"". American Nineteenth Century History.

Cleves, Rachel Hope; Eustace, Nicole; Gilje, Paul (September 2012). "Interchange: The War of 1812". Journal of American History.

Goodman, Warren H. (September 1941). "The Origins of the War of 1812: A Survey of Changing Interpretations". Mississippi Valley Historical Review.

Grodzinski, John R. (October 2012). "Opening Shots from the Bicentenary of the War of 1812: Canadian Perspective on Recent Titles". The Journal of Military History.

Hatter, Lawrence B.A. (Summer 2012). "Party Like It's 1812: The War at 200". Tennessee Historical Quarterly.

Hickey, Donald R. (September 2013). "1812: The Old History and the New". Reviews in American History.

Hickey, Donald R. (2001). "The War of 1812: Still a Forgotten Conflict?". The Journal of Military History.

Jensen, Richard (October 2012). "Military History on the Electronic Frontier: Wikipedia Fights the War of 1812" (PDF). The Journal of Military History.

Nivola, Pietro S.; Kastor, Peter J., eds. (2012). What So Proudly We Hailed: Essays on the Contemporary Meanings of the War of 1812. Brookings Institution Press.

Stacey, C.P. (1964). "The War of 1812 in Canadian History". In Zaslow; Morris; Turner, Wesley B (eds.). The Defended Border: Upper Canada and the War of 1812. Toronto: MacMillan.

Trautsch, Jasper M. (January 2013). "The Causes of the War of 1812: 200 Years of Debate" (PDF). The Journal of Military History.

G1 - 0146827

Manufactured by Amazon.ca
Bolton, ON